Dear Class

Traveling Around the World with Mrs. J

Jane J. Stein

Illustrated by Pamela A. Duckworth

Montview Press

DEDICATION

Happy Travels to
Sadie, Petra and Gavin Leite
Lydia and Eliza Stein

Published by Montview Press, Washington, DC

www.dearclassbook.com
dearclassbook@gmail.com

Stein, Jane J.
Dear Class: Traveling Around the World with Mrs. J

ISBN: 978-0-9961005-1-9 hardcover
ISBN: 978-0-9961005-0-2 paperback

Library of Congress Control Number: 20149087111

Book design: *design*Mind, Marianne Michalakis
Illustrations are watercolor and pen and ink on paper.

Table of Contents

In the Beginning

Mrs. J's fifth-grade class knew something was about to happen when she came to school one day talking with a newly acquired British accent and wearing a French beret. The students just weren't sure what would happen...or when.

After reading a story about children in Paris, Mrs. J made herself clear. "I'm going around the world next year, and I want you to guess my first two stops," she said. "I have actually given you hints about this."

Hmmm. New accent. Beret. This was going to be easy. "England and France," the class yelled out.

Mrs. J had always dreamed of traveling around the world. As a child, she read books about girls and boys living in different countries and imagined what life might be like there. She wanted to find out first-hand, but there always seemed to be something in the way. When she was in her twenties she didn't have enough money. When she was in her thirties she was newly married and had young children. When she was in her forties she was saving money for her children's college education. Even so, Mrs. J never gave up her dream of traveling around the world. She knew that one day she would do it.

This is the true story about how Mrs. J lived out her dream in 1963 when she was fifty-four years old. Her daughters had graduated from college. One had already traveled to Europe twice, while Mrs. J had been out of the country only to go north to Canada for a week and south to Mexico for a few days for a divorce.

Now was the time for her to travel. It was the time for her to have tea in London; to stand under the Eiffel Tower in Paris; to see Hindu temples in India and Buddhist pagodas in Thailand; and to sail on the Aegean Sea in Greece, the Black Sea in Turkey, and the Inland Sea in Japan.

Before she could do this, she had to convince the principal of her school to let her take six months off from teaching. She knew this would not be easy. International travel was different back in the early 1960s. Fewer Americans went abroad than do today, and even fewer women went by themselves. There were not as many airline connections from one city or country to another. And since Mrs. J was going to make hotel reservations only a day or two before arriving in a new city, no one would know where to send letters to her. Remember, there was no Internet, e-mail, texting, or tweeting back then.

None of this stopped Mrs. J. If she had a dream to live out—no matter how hard it would be—she would find a way to do it.

And she did.

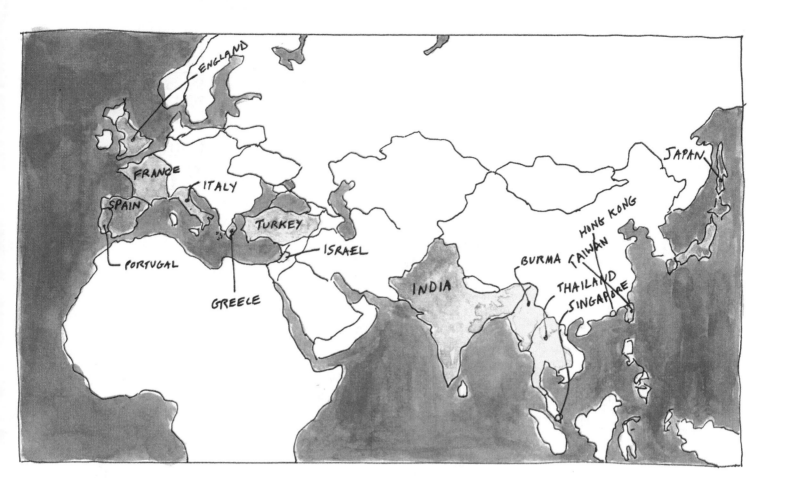

She got her school's approval to go on the trip and then bought an around-the-world airplane ticket. It was an open ticket, which meant she could go almost anywhere she wanted whenever she wanted—as long as it was within a year. She got a passport, visas for entry into some countries, immunizations required by others, and she was ready to go.

Mrs. J's parting words to her students were: "I'll write a letter to you from each country I visit so you can read about my adventures."

This plan sounded easy when she said it, but it actually required what Mrs. J called "thinking cap" time. "Since I am starting my trip just when you begin your summer vacation, if I write to you at school, no one will be there to read my letters over the summer," she said. "It's time to put on my thinking cap."

"Aha, the solution," she exclaimed, after a few seconds. "I'll send them to Mr. B, the principal, and someone from the Geography Club can pick up the letters at his house."

"This way," she said, "members of the club can read my letters, follow on a map where I've been, learn more about each country, and get a head start on preparing for the National Geographic Bee. The rest of the class can read the letters after school begins in the fall."

It's time to get on a magic carpet and travel around the world with Mrs. J.

This book is based on Mrs. J's letters and her travel notes. It also includes updates from the 1960s, fun facts, websites, art and cooking projects, and more.

Letter from **England**

July 3, 1963

Dear Class:

I've been in London for a week and already feel British. That's because—like many people here—I always go out with my umbrella. It is cold and foggy and has rained almost every day. But I'm off to see the world, even if I see it from under an umbrella.

I saw the Changing of the Guard at Buckingham Palace, climbed the Tower of London where heads rolled, heard Big Ben chime, and had tea in cozy little tea shops. One was even called The Cozy Tea Shoppe.

I love walking around cities, and London is great for that. But there is one problem. Because cars drive on the left side of the road—what we call the wrong side—crossing the street can be very dangerous. It seems like I was always looking for traffic in the wrong direction. Here's how I learned to cross the streets: Walk very close to someone who talks with a British accent and assume that he or she lives here and knows how to do it safely.

One of the fun things I did as I walked around the city was to look for unusual names of streets. Friday Street is named after the fishmongers who sold fish there on Fridays. There's a Man in the Moon

Big Ben is the largest four-faced chiming clock in the world. Built in 1859, it is in a tower at the end of the Parliament building. There are at least two different versions of how Big Ben got its name. One is that it is named after Sir Benjamin Hall, who oversaw the installation of the clock. The other is that it is named after a popular heavyweight fighter at the time, Benjamin Caunt. In any case, it was renamed the Elizabeth Tower in 2012 to honor Queen Elizabeth II's sixty years on the throne. See Mrs. J under her umbrella in front of Big Ben.

Buckingham Palace

The Queen's home in London is Buckingham Palace. Outside, guards dressed in red tunics, black pants, and tall furry hats change troops with all the formality you expect from royalty. You can smile at the guards, but they are trained never to smile back. All Mrs. J could think of when she was there was the A.A. Milne poem: "They're changing Guard at Buckingham Palace— Christopher Robin went down with Alice." (Milne also wrote *Winnie the Pooh*.)

Passage and Bleeding Heart Yard, which may have been the scene of a murder in 1626. To lighten things up, there is also a Ha Ha Road. My favorite name, though, is Petticoat Lane Market, where people sell clothes–in addition to petticoats, which are old-fashioned skirts often with ruffles and lace that were worn under dresses–from stalls on the street.

Speaking of walking: For more than a thousand years, kings, queens, soldiers, and clergy walked the aisles of Westminster Abbey. And now, so did I. There is so much to see–the stained glass windows, the paintings on the wall, and the Poets' Corner where many famous British writers are buried–that I didn't know where to look first. I chose the Poets' Corner.

The Abbey has been the burial place for royalty since the eleventh century. It also is the place where great celebrations for the living are held, such as coronations and royal weddings. Queen Elizabeth II was crowned in the Abbey in 1953, and I watched it on TV. I stood just where she did, and I actually felt queenly. Maybe that's because my childhood name was Queenie.

The British Museum, founded in 1753, is the oldest public museum in the world and is free to all

Tower of London

William the Conqueror built a fortress to guard the entrance to London soon after he became king in 1066. Although the fortress is called the Tower of London, it actually has 21 towers. Over the centuries, the Tower of London was used as a royal palace, a treasury, and a prison. Princes and queens as well as thieves were hanged, burned, and beheaded behind the fortress walls. A more pleasant thing to do there today is to see the dazzling crown jewels.

"studious and curious persons." This sounds like the place for me! It houses objects thousands of years old, including the skin of a two thousand-year-old human found in a swamp in England and mummies of cats (humans, too) from ancient Egypt. You know how I love books, so a special treat for me was to see the beautifully displayed original manuscripts. <u>Jane Eyre</u>, a nineteenth-century novel by Charlotte Brontë, was opened to a very dramatic part of the story, where the wedding between Jane and Rochester was halted because he was still married to a crazy woman who lived in the attic.

London is well known for its theater, so I made sure to see a play one evening. We get our theater programs for free in the United States, so I was surprised that here you have to pay for one. Much to my embarrassment, I didn't have enough English pounds with me—that is English money, not the extra weight I gained eating pastries with my tea.

As much fun as I had in London, I took a trip out of town for a day. I caught a train at Paddington Station (that is the station Paddington Bear was named after because the book's author lived near it) and ended up in Stratford-upon-Avon, where the countryside is

At the time of Mrs. J's trip, getting money to use in the country you were visiting wasn't as easy as it is today, when you can get local currency from an ATM (automated teller machine). At that time, many Americans had special travelers checks that were converted to the country's currency at banks and stores. Britain still uses the pound, but starting in 2002, many European countries stopped using their own currency and started using the euro. When Mrs. J was in France, she used francs; in Italy, lira; in Portugal, escudos; in Spain, pesos; and in Greece, drachmas. Today, she would use euros in all those places. This is a lot easier than learning a different money system in each country.

British Museum

The manuscripts Mrs. J saw at the British Museum are now housed in a new building of the British Library. The library has so many items—books, stamps, maps, manuscripts—that if you saw five items a day, it would take eighty thousand years to see the whole collection.

About the cat mummies at the British Museum: Egyptians did not worship animals, but many of their gods and goddesses had their own specific animals. The cat was the special animal to the goddess Bastet. Back then, some people believed that if you left a cat mummy at her temple, Bastet would help solve your problems. Do you think this would really work?

lush and there are flowers everywhere. It should be lush because of all the rain.

Stratford-upon-Avon is the birthplace of William Shakespeare and home of the Swan Theater where the Royal Shakespeare Theater performs his plays. I saw <u>The Tempest</u>, which is a fantasy about love, magic, power, and forgiveness. Seeing it performed in England—and particularly in Stratford—the play made more sense to me than when I saw it in New York. Even for a teacher, Shakespeare's words can sometimes be hard to follow.

In addition to visiting Shakespeare's birthplace, I went to the cottage where his wife, Anne Hathaway, grew up. It still has some of the original sixteenth-century furniture, including the bed she slept in. The guides wore clothing from Anne and Will's time. It was so real-looking that I expected to see Shakespeare himself knock on the front door. I was not surprised to learn that Stratford is the most visited tourist attraction in England outside London.

On my last day in London I went to the Tate Gallery. It turns out that I saved the best for last.

Tate Modern

Today, there is another Tate in London—the Tate Modern, housed in an old power station on the banks of the River Thames. Mrs. J would have loved the modern art there. A boat takes people from one Tate to another. Doesn't that sound like a fun way to go to a museum?

In 2011, Queen Elizabeth's grandson, William, married Kate Middleton in Westminster Abbey. More than three billion people watched the wedding on TV. Did you see it?

The Tate has a lot of paintings by my favorite British artist, William Turner. He always loved drawing. When he was thirteen, his father sold his son's paintings at his barber shop. Then, only two years later, Turner was exhibiting at the Royal Academy of Arts. That's quite a jump for a teenage artist—from a barber shop to the Royal Academy.

I cancelled plans to visit Parliament (the line was too long) and take another look around Westminster Abbey (it was too rainy). Maybe I'm just too excited about where I'll be tomorrow: PARIS.

Farewell to London,

Mrs. J

If You Go to London...

- What would you want to see first in London? The cat mummies at the British Museum or the Tower of London, where people had their heads chopped off?

- Harry Potter wasn't written when Mrs. J took her trip so she didn't know about checking out Platform 9¾ at Kings Cross Station. Even though it doesn't really exist, don't you want to go to the station just to make sure? So many people go to check on this that there is a Platform 9¾ sign on a wall close to the real platform

Fun Facts:
Did You Know That...

- London Bridge—as in "London Bridge is falling down, falling down"— isn't in London anymore. It crosses the Bridgewater Channel in Lake Havasu City, Arizona.

- If you are hungry for a special British dish, you can try bury black pudding, which is made from jellied pig's blood and oatmeal. Maybe it tastes better than it sounds.

- There are traffic lights in London for horses. Actually, they are for people riding horses. Buttons are placed at higher-than-pedestrian height for riders to push to make the lights change so they can cross the street safely.

- Athelhampton House in Dorset is supposed to be the most haunted place in England. One of the ghosts is reported to be a pet ape that got trapped in a secret passage. Some people say they hear the ape scratching on the wall to escape. What do you think this sounds like?

Check Out What Mrs. J Saw: AN ONLINE TOUR

Big Ben: www.parliament.uk/bigben
British Museum: www.britishmuseum.org
Changing the Guard at Buckingham Palace:
 www.royal.gov.uk/RoyalEventsandCeremonies/ChangingtheGuard/overview.aspx
Tate Gallery: www.tate.org.uk
Westminster Abbey: www.westminster-abbey.org

Something British *for* You to Do

ENGLAND Word Search

T	C	E	E	G	Y	A	Z	T	D	K	X	K	D	T
Y	A	J	R	J	R	J	B	R	V	I	X	X	G	U
L	B	H	L	A	F	P	O	W	P	T	O	D	N	B
C	H	Y	S	Z	E	F	W	T	D	E	Y	R	I	L
H	Z	R	M	K	T	P	H	Y	D	E	P	A	R	K
I	G	C	P	A	V	E	S	E	Z	B	Z	U	Q	M
P	T	A	R	C	N	B	H	E	I	M	D	G	O	N
S	H	T	T	E	D	Q	B	T	K	C	R	B	X	Y
Y	S	R	B	W	G	Y	K	F	W	A	P	E	I	N
J	M	G	S	B	U	C	K	I	N	G	H	A	M	E
X	I	L	O	N	D	O	N	R	J	C	X	S	J	B
B	T	W	N	A	C	Z	K	Q	E	H	S	I	F	R
C	A	N	C	O	B	R	I	T	I	S	H	I	C	J
B	C	B	J	X	K	T	D	F	H	Y	H	R	G	M
N	O	T	G	N	I	D	D	A	P	N	E	E	U	Q

Find these hidden words in the grid.

They can be horizontal, vertical, or diagonal and frontward or backward. Mrs. J saw things related to or ate everything on this list. The British call French fries "chips." Fish and chips is a popular dish in England. *The solution is on page 80.*

BIG BEN	HYDE PARK
BRITISH	LONDON
BUCKINGHAM	QUEEN
CHIPS	PADDINGTON
FISH	SHAKESPEARE
GUARD	STRATFORD

Letter from
France

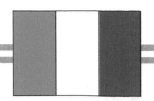

Mrs. J in her room in Paris

August 14, 1963

Dear Class:

I LOVE PARIS.

Lucky me, I spent six weeks in Paris. On my first day there I walked along the Seine, the river that separates the city into the Left Bank and the Right Bank. In between are some islands, including the Île de la Cité, where Notre Dame Cathedral soars up into the sky. I could see the tower where the famous hunchback of Notre Dame from Victor Hugo's novel swung from the bells. But there was no sign of the hunchback or Madeline, her classmates, and the stern Miss Clavel. (Remember the line from the children's book about Madeline? "In an old house in Paris that was covered with vines, lived twelve little girls in two straight lines.")

I wandered inside Notre Dame and sat down to rest my feet and look at the beautiful paintings, sculptures, and stained-glass windows. To my surprise and delight, I found my way back to my room—a charming place with a small balcony and a table where I had fresh croissants and coffee for breakfast every day.

Paris is beautiful at night, with many of the buildings and the Eiffel Tower lit up. It was especially bright on the night of July 14 because of fireworks.

Notre Dame

Construction of Notre Dame, one of the great cathedrals of the world, started in the twelfth century and was completed in the fourteenth century. The gargoyles (a cross between a dragon and a prehistoric bird) were added in the nineteenth century. Technically, they aren't even gargoyles, which are sculpted figures that act as waterspouts; the ones on Notre Dame are just for show and are called grotesques.

(July 14 is the French national holiday that celebrates the beginning of the French Revolution with the storming of the Bastille prison in 1789.) People were dancing in the streets, and one group asked me to join them. I'm not a great dancer, but everyone was having so much fun that no one noticed.

Have you ever heard of a busman's holiday? That's when a bus driver takes a driving trip for a vacation. Well, I did something like that. I am a school teacher and spent six weeks of my vacation going to the Sorbonne, the most famous university in France. I studied French—the first time since college classes thirty years ago—and I did much better than I thought I would. One day we had a new teacher who talked <u>très vite</u>—very fast—but I still understood her. There were twenty other students in the class from many different countries, including Italy, Colombia, Denmark, and Algeria. Even though I left the United States only six weeks ago, I have already gotten to know people from all corners of the earth.

After class, I had lunch and sometimes went to American Express to check for mail, but almost every day I went to a museum. The first time I saw the <u>Winged Victory of Samothrace</u> at the Louvre I almost couldn't believe I was really seeing it. I felt that

Eiffel Tower

Built for the Universal Exhibition of 1889, the Eiffel Tower (named for Gustave Eiffel, the architect who designed it) was supposed to stand for twenty years, but it became a symbol of Paris and was never torn down. When built, it was the tallest structure in the world (1,063 feet). Today, the tallest building—in Dubai, the United Arab Emirates—is more than twice as high.

I'd been waiting for that moment all of my life. A huge marble sculpture created in the second century B.C., Miss Victory has outstretched wings and dominates the stairway where she is placed. As big as the space is, she looks so cramped there.

My next stop in the Louvre was to see <u>Venus de Milo</u>, another larger-than-life Greek sculpture. She looks so lovely and peaceful in spite of not having any arms and having to put up with so many visitors and noisy guides around her.

When I wasn't in a museum, I explored Paris and its wonderful street life.

- Montmartre is like an open-air art studio with artists selling paintings, sketching portraits of tourists, and drawing scenes of Paris in chalk on the sidewalk. I have taken a lot of painting classes and tried to imagine myself as an artist, but decided I am happier being a school teacher.
- Shopping in a flea market is always fun. The big one in Paris is called Marché aux Puces. <u>Puces</u> is the French word for fleas. What is junk for one person is a find for another. I bought an old guidebook to France to learn more about different parts of the country and also to practice reading French.

In life before e-mail, getting regular mail abroad was a challenge for tourists. Most Americans had mail sent to them at an American Express or airline office in a city where they planned to be.

The Louvre is one of the most famous museums of the world. Leonardo da Vinci's *Mona Lisa*—the lady who looks like she is smiling directly at you— is one of the greatest attractions there. Mrs. J spent half an hour looking at her, but other visitors spend more time having their picture taken in front of her than actually looking at her. See all the tourists looking at the *Winged Victory of Samothrace* on the right.

On the weekends, when there was no school, I took trips out of town. One weekend, I went to Normandy and saw the famous Bayeux Tapestry. (Actually, it is a very long piece of embroidered cloth; a tapestry is woven.) It tells the story of how William, the Duke of Normandy in France, conquered England in 1066. After that, he was called William the Conqueror. His coronation at Westminster Abbey took place soon after the Battle of Hastings, which is shown in the tapestry. Remember my telling you about my walking down the aisle of Westminster Abbey? At the time I wrote that, I didn't know that William the Conqueror had walked there, too.

In nearby Rouen, I saw the cathedral that the artist Claude Monet painted more than thirty times between 1892 and 1894. It's not that he couldn't get it right the first time. He just wanted to show how the light would look if he painted it at different times of the day and year and in different weather conditions. These paintings are in museums around the world. While in Rouen, I threw some flowers on the Joan of Arc memorial on the site where she was burned at the stake in 1431. It was raining only slightly that day—not enough to put out a fire for poor Joan.

Joan of Arc is a French heroine and Catholic saint. She led the French to victory over the English in the fifteenth century, but was later sold to the English and tried for crimes against the church. One crime was wearing men's clothing when she fought in battle. She was sentenced to die by burning.

Another weekend I visited chateaux—very large country houses—in the Loire Valley, which is south of Paris in the center of France. (Chateaux is the plural of chateau.) One chateau, Chenonceau, is like a fairy-tale castle. The Bedroom of the Five Queens was used at different times by five young women who went on to become queens in France or Spain. Now that's a fairy tale come true.

Back to real life, I stopped at an open-air market in a tiny nearby village where people were selling fresh everything—from fruits and vegetables to live chickens. I bought fresh bread at a boulangerie (bakery), a great cheese at a fromagerie (cheese store), and delicious sliced ham at a charcuterie (place to buy salamis, sausages, and what we call deli meats).

I saved all of these goodies for dinner in my room and ate lunch in a café. A nice lady who served me coffee graciously led me through her living room, out to the backyard to the outhouse. Hanging on a nail was what I was supposed to use for toilet paper: sheets of newspaper. This is why I was told always to travel with my own TP.

When my classes were over, I had a few days to go to places I hadn't visited yet. A short train ride from

Chenonceau was built in the sixteenth century and had lots of owners over the years. In 1650, King Louis XIV visited his uncle who was living there. As a thank-you-for-the-visit present, the king sent him furniture covered in priceless silk. Some thank-you present!

Paris brought me to the Palace of Versailles, which had housed kings, queens, emperors, and empresses. It is a popular place to visit. The day I was there it was very crowded. After touring the palace, I escaped the hordes of people by walking to <u>Le Hameau</u> (The Little Hamlet), a rustic retreat complete with a farmhouse, dairy, mill, birdhouse, and more. It was built for Queen Marie Antoinette, who also wanted to get away from the crowds at Versailles.

I'm off to Italy tomorrow, and after that I don't know where I'll go or when. I've seen young people all summer jumping from place to place without reservations. If they can do it, I can, too.

<u>Au revoir</u> (pronounced o-ruh-vwar) to Paris,

Mrs. J

Versailles

What started out as a hunting lodge ended up as one of the largest palaces in the world. Versailles has everything, including an opera house, chapels, gardens, and lots and lots of rooms. One of the most famous rooms is the Hall of Mirrors, which has more than 350 mirrors. This was a very big deal in the seventeenth century when Versailles was built. Mirrors were very expensive then, and even kings and queens usually didn't have many.

If You Go to Paris...

- Mrs. J liked to go to art museums, but there are many museums in Paris that specialize in offbeat things, including circus art, fashion, film, and magic. Which museum would you visit?

- There are lots of ways to travel around the city—walking, biking, taking the Metro (the subway), buses, and even boats. How would you like to see Paris?

Fun Facts:
Did You Know That...

- The Statue of Liberty, a gift of friendship from France to the United States, has been in the New York harbor since 1886. There are three smaller models of it in Paris. One is in the Luxembourg Gardens near the Sorbonne, where Mrs. J went to school.

- *Franglais* is when a word or phrase is made up of some French and a lot of English, as in *le weekend*, *le blue jeans*, *c'est cool* (that's cool).

- The milk you drink every day is safe because of a Frenchman. Louis Pasteur found that tiny things called microbes live in milk and other food products and can cause disease. Heat kills off the microbes in a process called pasteurization.

- Paris specializes in showing off its sewers. On what is sometimes called the Bad Taste Tour, you can visit this vast underground world. Among unusual items found there have been teeth and a crocodile.

Check Out What Mrs. J Saw: AN ONLINE TOUR

Chenonceau: www.chenonceau.com
Eiffel Tower: www.tour-eiffel.fr
Louvre: www.louvre.fr (click on translate for English)
Notre Dame Cathedral: www.notredamedeparis.fr
Versailles: en.chateauversailles.fr

16

Something French *for* You to Do

Make a *Croque Monsieur*

A *Croque Monsieur* is a popular fast food or snack in France. It is basically a grilled ham and cheese sandwich, but its French name makes it sound fancier. *Croque* means crunch so it literally translates as a crunchy man.

Here's how to make one:

Ingredients (for 2 sandwiches)

4 slices of white bread
2 tablespoons of butter
2 slices of ham
2 slices of cheese

Instructions

1. Cut the crusts off the bread.

2. Butter the bread on both sides.

3. Put a slice of ham and cheese between two pieces of bread.

4. Melt the remaining butter in a pan and put the sandwiches in the pan.

5. When the bottom slice of bread is golden, turn the sandwiches over with a spatula.

6. Fry on the other side until golden.

7. Cut in half and serve.

Variation:
A *Croque Madame* is the same as a *Croque Monsieur* but has a fried or poached egg on top.

September 6, 1963

Dear Class:

I arrived in Milan on a national holiday in Italy, and all of the museums were closed. As you know, I love seeing art, so I was very disappointed at first. But I got to see one of the most famous paintings in the world anyway—Leonardo da Vinci's <u>Last Supper</u>—by going into the Santa Maria delle Grazie Monastery. (I saw his painting, <u>Mona Lisa</u>, at the Louvre in Paris.) <u>The Last Supper</u> was painted directly on a huge wall of the monastery's dining room. The painting is hard to see because so much of it has either faded or totally disappeared. The lighting is also poor. Even so, it's where da Vinci painted it. He didn't realize how many people would want to see it centuries later.

I wandered into the Duomo, which is the largest cathedral in Italy. It is so big that it can hold forty thousand people. Remember when I read stories to you by Mark Twain? Well, when Twain visited Milan in 1867, he couldn't get over how big the cathedral was and at the same time so airy and graceful. I agree with him!

The next day, when public buildings were open, I went to La Scala—one of the great opera houses of

The Last Supper
started to flake less than twenty years after da Vinci finished painting it in 1498. Parts of it have been redone over the centuries, including a restoration completed in 1999 to repair areas where the paint had flaked and to remove layers of earlier restorations, which were eating away the original paint. The colors are much brighter today than when Mrs. J saw it. The restoration took twenty years because some days the work completed was only the size of a postage stamp. Da Vinci did the original painting over a three-year period.

the world. Even though there are no performances in the summer, I took a tour of the building and went into the glistening gold-and-white mirrored lobby. I also went backstage, which is big enough to hold a chorus of eight hundred singers. I remember my father telling me about his days on the stage of the Metropolitan Opera in New York. He didn't sing a word, which is a good thing because he had a terrible voice. He was an extra or what in the opera world is called a supernumerary. Extras usually are just part of a crowd scene.

I traveled a lot by train in Italy—from Milan all the way down to Naples with stops in between. The first stop was Venice. The Grand Canal is the main waterway in Venice. In fact, it's like Main Street except it's not on dry land. How lucky for me that the patio of my hotel faced it. The patio also faced a lovely church. One morning I saw a bride get out of a special Venetian boat called a gondola and go up the canal stairs that led to the church for her wedding. She didn't even get her feet wet!

The <u>vaporetto</u> or water bus goes up and down the Grand Canal and also to nearby islands. I went to Murano, which is known for making glass beads and figurines, and to Torcello, where I visited two old

The Grand Canal

forms a giant S from one end of Venice to the other—from the railroad station, which is on the mainland, to St. Mark's Square. Venice is made up of more than a hundred islands separated by canals and linked by bridges. There are no streets or cars in the city. The only way to get anywhere is by walking or taking a boat. There are water buses, police boats, fire boats, and ambulance boats.

Bridge of Sighs

The most famous bridge in Venice is the Bridge of Sighs, built in 1602 to connect the old prison and interrogation rooms in the Doge's Palace (he was the head of the Republic of Venice) with the new prison on the other side of a canal. The bridge got its name, according to one story, because people who passed from the old prison to the new one—and possibly to their execution— sighed at seeing what could be their last view of Venice. A more romantic story about the bridge's name is that a couple will have everlasting love if they kiss in a gondola at sunset under the bridge. In this case, the sighs come from lovers, not prisoners. Mrs. J took a gondola ride one afternoon and went under the bridge.

Baptistry of San Giovanni

One of the oldest buildings in Florence is the Baptistry of San Giovanni, built in the eleventh century. It is famous for its bronze doors, called the Gates of Paradise, which were added in the fifteenth century. The sculptures on the door portray ten biblical stories, including Adam and Eve, Moses and the Ten Commandments, and David and Goliath. Mrs. J saw the original doors, (see illustration on the left) but now they are in a nearby museum. The doors on the Baptistry today are copies.

churches from the seventh and eleventh centuries. A long time ago, more people lived in Torcello than in Venice. Over the years, however, the island became swampland and the population dwindled. Today very few people live there.

It is always fun for me to walk around cities, and Venice was no different—except there are no traffic lights or big streets to cross. I loved wandering around the back alleys away from the busy Grand Canal. The buildings are very old, many of them dating back to the sixteenth century. Except for my modern-day clothing, I felt like I could be part of a street scene from Shakespeare's <u>Merchant of Venice</u>.

Working my way south by train, my next stop was Florence. One way I learn about a new city is to take a half-day tour of it. That way, I can see where I want to spend more time. I was glad I spent a few days in Florence because there are so many beautiful buildings and so much beautiful art there.

The highlight of art viewing for me in Florence was the Uffizi Gallery, where one of my favorite paintings hangs—Sandro Botticelli's <u>Birth of Venus</u>. In this painting, Venus—the goddess of love and beauty—emerges from the sea standing on a giant shell. I

The Forum was the center of Roman public life from the seventh century B.C. to the sixth century A.D. What were once streets crowded with government buildings and temples is now a grassy area of ruins with just a hint of what the structures might have looked like. Some of the columns still stand, but many lie in pieces on the ground.

remember when I saw it at the Metropolitan Museum of Art in New York, where it came for a tour during World War II. I never imagined that I would see it again, yet there I was face-to-face with gorgeous Venus.

I arrived in Rome on my birthday. What a great place to celebrate! There is so much to see just walking down the street. Ruins from ancient Rome are tucked in between modern buildings. There also are a lot of fountains-not ones to drink from but ones with huge sculptures spewing water. In the Trevi Fountain, Neptune, the god of the sea, is riding a chariot in the shape of a shell that is pulled by two horses. There is a legend that people who throw coins into this fountain will come back to Rome. I'm not usually superstitious, but I threw in a coin because I definitely want to come back. So do a lot of people because about three thousand coins are tossed into the fountain every day!

Speaking of coming back, my Latin from high school classes came back when I walked through the Forum, just as my French did in Paris. I recited some of the famous sayings of Julius Caesar, standing on the very spot where he stood more than two thousand years ago, and I went back one evening for a sound and light show. For the light part, the buildings in the

Forum are lit up. For the sound part, there is music and a recorded story of what took place there. The show made history come alive, and I could imagine famous Romans walking around there in their togas. Remember when we made togas out of sheets for a Roman party last year?

I loved being in Rome for many reasons, but especially because it's where I went to an opera. What a spectacle it was—<u>Aida</u> performed in the Baths of Caracalla. In addition to the singers, there were elephants, camels, and horses on stage. While it's used for opera today, the Baths of Caracalla were "the" place to take a bath in third-century A.D. Rome. Maybe the idea of reading in the bathtub came from here because these baths had not one library but two-one for Greek literature, the other for Latin.

Continuing on south, I went to Pompeii, the city that was buried in volcanic ash after Mt. Vesuvius blew up in 79 A.D. and was abandoned for centuries. It wasn't until 1748 that explorers rediscovered Pompeii lying under the dust and debris. Much to everyone's surprise, it looked just as it did before the volcano erupted. At one home you can even see a dog who couldn't escape because he was tied up.

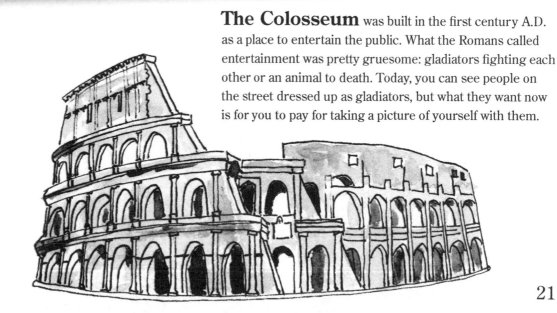

The Colosseum was built in the first century A.D. as a place to entertain the public. What the Romans called entertainment was pretty gruesome: gladiators fighting each other or an animal to death. Today, you can see people on the street dressed up as gladiators, but what they want now is for you to pay for taking a picture of yourself with them.

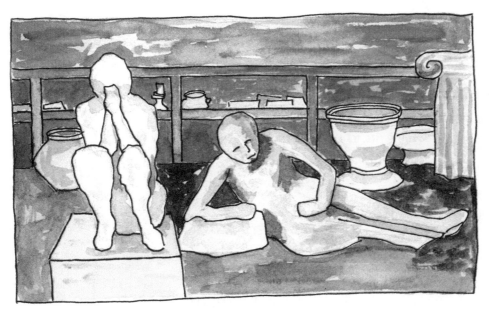

Body casts of people buried in Pompeii

My tour of Italy ended with a drive from Naples along the shore of the Mediterranean Sea to Sorrento, a beautiful town on top of cliffs. On nearby Isle of Capri, I rode on a chair lift to the summit of Mount Solaro, the highest place on the island. I was scared at first because I was so far off the ground, I felt like I was dangling in the air. Once I was at the top I was glad I did it. Not only were the views of the sea spectacular, but also there were ruins of an ancient Greek home, pool, and garden. What a luxurious life they led. At least they weren't buried in ash like their neighbors in Pompeii.

After my last pasta dinner in Italy, I packed for my next adventure in Portugal and Spain.

Ciao (pronounced chow) to Italy,

Mrs. J

If You Go to Italy...

- What would you eat first: pizza or gelato (ice cream)? *See the first Fun Facts.*

- How would you say your name in Italian?

Fun Facts:
Did You Know That...

- Pizza might have been eaten in Italy as long ago as ancient Rome, but the world's first pizzeria opened in Naples in 1830. What's your favorite pizza? Another Italian food invention is the gelato cone. What's your favorite flavor?

- Rome is farther north than New York City, but it snows in Rome only once every several years. New Yorkers have to dig cars from snowbanks almost every year.

- The most popular girls' names in Italy today are Giulia and Martina. The most popular boys' names are Francesco and Alessandro.

- Vatican City, the home of the Catholic Church, is an independent state within Italy. It is the only nation in the world that can lock its gates at night. It has its own phone company, radio, TV station, currency, passports, and stamps.

Check Out What Mrs. J Saw: AN ONLINE TOUR

Accademia and Uffizi Galleries: www.polomuseale.firenze.it
(click on the British flag for English)
Grand Canal: www.aviewoncities.com/venice/canalgrande.htm
The Last Supper: www.sacred-destinations.com/italy/milan-santa-maria-delle-grazie-last-supper
Pompeii: www.eyewitnesstohistory.com/pompeii.htm
Roman Forum: www.rome.info/roman-forum

Something Italian *for* You to Do

Have a Pizza Party

Do you like pizza? What topping is your favorite? Cheese? Pepperoni? Onions? Mushrooms? Green peppers? Ham? Pineapple? Well, your favorite might not be what your best friend likes. Here's how to please everyone.

Invite a group of friends to a pizza party. You supply the crust and pizza sauce, and each person brings one or two toppings. Buy ready-made pizza crusts and a jar of sauce at the supermarket. Divide the crusts into sections. Each person gets to decorate a section with toppings. Cut the sections into pieces so everyone gets to taste all of the different pizzas.

You can make a game out of pizza making. Have teams of two people work together on a section. Again, cut the sections into pieces so everyone gets a taste of each slice. Then have your friends vote for the best-tasting pizza or the one with the weirdest toppings or whatever categories you want.

Every party needs dessert at the end, so why not make a dessert pizza? Prepare a brownie mix according to the instructions on the package. Pour the batter into a round pizza pan with sides or a different shallow pan. The batter will be spread fairly thin. so it will take less time to bake than usual. Bake the brownie until a toothpick inserted in the center comes out clean. After it cools, add toppings to make it a dessert pizza. Here are some topping ideas: crushed cookies or candy bars, whipped cream, and ice cream. What else would you add to a dessert pizza?

Letter from
Portugal and **Spain**

Lisbon

Most of the buildings in Lisbon were destroyed in 1755 by an earthquake, which also caused a tsunami (huge, rushing waves from the ocean) and fires. Mrs. J didn't know it when she was there, but she would have been saddened to learn that a new opera house was one of the casualties, and it burned to the ground. Lisbon was rebuilt with some of the first buildings in Europe designed to be safer in an earthquake.

September 22, 1963

Dear Class:

When I first came to the Iberian Peninsula—the part of Europe that includes Portugal and Spain—I felt like I was time-traveling back...and back...and back in history.

Maybe this was because the first thing I did after checking into my hotel in Lisbon, the capital of Portugal, was to walk to the National Museum of Ancient Art to see its collection going back to the fourteenth century. When a guard saw me admiring one of the paintings, he came over to talk to me about it. Since I don't speak Portuguese and he didn't speak English, we settled on having a conversation in French. He told me things about the painting and asked me questions about the United States. My teacher at the Sorbonne would have been very proud of me. Without those classes, I would not have had the confidence to talk to someone in French.

After exploring Lisbon, I took a day trip that went along the Atlantic coast—the Costa do Sol (Sunny Coast)—to Estoril, a fishing village that was famous as a seaside resort for royalty. In fact, King Umberto II of Italy came the same day I did. Actually, he was no longer the king because the monarchy was abolished in

1946, but he was still royalty. Am I in good company (or should I say is he is in good company)?

Leaving the coast, we went inland to Sintra, which has buildings ranging from eighth-century castles to a nineteenth-century royal summer retreat. The Palacio Nacional da Pena (Pena National Palace) sits on the top of a hill. On a clear day you can see Lisbon from it, and from Lisbon you can see the palace. While it wasn't raining the day I was there, it was very foggy so I didn't get much of a view. That was okay with me because the palace and gardens around it were worth the trip. After visiting here, Hans Christian Andersen said it was the most beautiful place in Portugal-like in a fairy tale. And he certainly knew a lot about fairy-tale places.

Now I'll tell you about some of the things that I saw from the way-back past when I was on a three-day tour through central Portugal on which I was the only person. A private tour on a school teacher's budget! What good luck for me that no one else signed up for it. The guide-Maria-was very good company, but the driver wasn't. There was a slow leak in a tire and he didn't want to repair it. We drove for an hour on a rough road to a town with a car repair shop. There was no mechanic at the shop so Mr. Driver had to fix the tire anyway.

Pena National Palace

The palace was originally painted in bright yellow and red. When Mrs. J was there, the colors had faded so it looked gray. Since then, the palace was repainted so it is colorful again.

Trash pick-up day in a Portuguese village

The Moors—Muslims from North Africa—invaded the Iberian Peninsula in 711. They ruled Portugal for centuries, but were defeated in 1249. Two and a half centuries later, in 1492, the Moors were defeated by Queen Isabella and King Ferdinand in Spain, the royal pair who sent Christopher Columbus on the trip when he found America.

While we were waiting, donkey- and horse-drawn carts carrying garbage passed by, as did women filling up tin cans at the water fountain. They put the cans filled with water on their heads. As if this wasn't heavy enough, one woman put two big boots on top of the cans. Here, people removed trash and got water just as they did hundreds of years ago.

After the tire was repaired, we drove past many walled cities. Some were built by Moors, some by Portuguese, but all were meant to protect against invasion from one group or another. The houses are centuries old and are still standing because they are made of stone. Inside the floors are dirt and outside the walls are whitewashed three or four times a year. Some people still have no indoor plumbing or a kitchen; they get water from a well or public fountain and cook on a charcoal fire outside the house.

Maria invited me to her cousin's house in a small village. Like the houses we saw in the walled cities, this was simple on the outside but modern inside. The kitchen was very large with a marble sink, an electric stove, and a refrigerator. Maria's family was very friendly. After giving me a cold drink, they showed me around the fields where women were weaving dried onion tops—with the onions still attached to them—into braids to sell at a fair. I know how to braid hair, so I asked if I could try it. One woman showed me how, but I quickly found out that braiding onions is much harder than braiding hair, and I gave up.

Speaking of fairs, we stopped in a town with one going on. As a special event, there were two bulls running loose around the town square. I was glad to be in a car and not on the street. Their horns looked sharp!

Back in Lisbon, I had trouble sleeping on my last night in Portugal. One reason was because I was excited about leaving for Spain. But another was that the wind was howling. It was so strong that it blew down a three hundred-year-old tree.

It was a plane, not the wind, that brought me to Madrid. After a quick stop at American Express to get mail, I did my usual half-day tour of the city. There are many parks in Madrid that we drove past, but we got off the bus to walk around the Parque del Retiro. Literally, this means a park where you can retreat or go to. In addition to people, ducks go to the park. I fed some of them crumbs from a roll I took from breakfast. The ducks snacked on it instead of me.

A highlight of the tour was a visit to the Palacio Real (Royal Palace), which has more than a thousand rooms. We saw thirty of them—enough for me to get

Mrs. J feeding ducks near the Crystal Palace in Madrid's Parque del Retiro

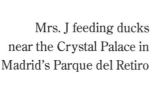

Mrs. J at the Fountain of Lions
in the Alhambra Palace

Seville Cathedral

One of the towers of the Seville cathedral was built originally as a minaret, which is the place where a muezzin calls Muslims to let them know it is time to pray. There is a ramp that goes up to the top so the muezzin can get up there by horseback. You can climb up by foot for a great view of Seville.

the feeling of over-the-top royal elegance. My whirlwind first day in Spain ended with dinner atop the tallest building for a good meal and a bird's-eye view of the city.

After a few days in Madrid, I toured the southern part of Spain, driving past olive trees, windmills, and walled cities to Granada and the famous Alhambra. The Alhambra—it's actually four buildings surrounded by magnificent gardens—was built by the Moors in the thirteenth century. Alhambra is Arabic for red because it was built using red earth and stone. The American author, Washington Irving, spent weeks here in 1829 and wrote <u>Tales of the Alhambra</u>. One of the stories tells about girls dancing in a courtyard for the sultan—the Muslim ruler—while blind musicians performed on the balcony. (Blind musicians were used so they wouldn't see the girls.) And there I was—standing where they danced!

What could be more of a contrast to the splendor of Alhambra than our next stop—gypsy homes in caves. The gypsies sang and performed dances for us (and passed a hat for money afterward).

Heading south, we went to Seville. The cathedral, which was built over a mosque, has many gold and jeweled treasures, including a sculpture of Our Lady of Sorrows, whose tears are real diamonds. It is known

"The rain in Spain falls mainly on the plain" is a line from the musical *My Fair Lady*. Mrs. J kept thinking of that song because it rained a lot when she was there. The good thing about the rain is that it cooled down the temperature. There is a place in Spain called Devil's Kitchen, where it can get so hot in the summer that people say you can fry eggs on the road. Which would you prefer: rain or very hot weather?

as the bullfighters' church because it is where they pray for a good fight—good for them at least, not the bulls. I didn't go to a bullfight, but I did visit a bull ring where young boys were learning how to be bullfighters. They were practicing with cows and used darts instead of swords. I felt sorry for one of the cows when a boy got it on the side with a dart. Imagine how I would feel if I saw a bull getting gored by a sword!

For my last night on the road trip, I stayed in a castle—a real fifteenth-century one. The Oropesa Castle was home for the Counts of Toledo but it also housed visiting soldiers, priests, and nobles. Now it houses tourists like me. The courtyard was used for jousting contests—when two knights on horses charged each other with sharp lances to knock each other to the ground. It was like fencing on horses.

Back in Madrid, I had planned a farewell dinner with friends whom I've made along the way, but we couldn't find a restaurant open at the time we wanted to eat. In Spain, dinner usually starts at ten p.m. I tumbled into bed after saying goodbye to a friend from Johannesburg, who gave me her address in case my travels take me to South Africa some day. Tomorrow is Greece!

<u>Adeus</u> (pronounced a-dew) to Portugal, <u>adios</u> (pronounced a-th-yaws) to Spain,

Mrs. J

Mrs. J never went to South Africa, but she did travel to Morocco in North Africa. She eventually visited all the continents of the world except Antarctica: North America, South America, Africa, Europe, Asia, and Australia.

If You Go to Portugal or Spain...

- Do you want to go to a bullfight? In Portugal it is against the law to kill a bull in the arena. Instead, it is killed by a professional butcher away from the audience. In Spain, the kill takes place in front of the audience.

- It is fun to stay overnight in a real castle. Many of them are now hotels and are called *pousadas* in Portugal and *paradors* in Spain.

Fun Facts: Did You Know That...

- There is a hidden Roman world underneath the streets of Lisbon, which was discovered after the 1755 earthquake. It is open to visitors only two days a year.

- To get from one level to another in the hilly city of Lisbon, you can take a cable car, an escalator, or an elevator. The elevator is in a tower created by Eiffel, who knew something about building towers.

- There is no tooth fairy in Spain, but there is a tooth mouse—Ratoncito Pérez.

- The world's largest tomato fight—La Tomatina—takes place the last Wednesday in August in Buñol, a small town in eastern Spain. Some 150,000 tomatoes are thrown at anyone and anything in sight for a messy—a very messy—half-hour of fun.

Check Out What Mrs. J Saw: AN ONLINE TOUR

Alhambra: www.greatbuildings.com/buildings/The_Alhambra.html
La Tomatina—the tomato fight: www.latomatina.org
National Museum of Ancient Art: www.museudearteantiga.pt (click on translate for English)
Pena National Palace: www.historiadeportugal.info/parque-e-palacio-da-pena
  (click on translate for English)
Prado Museum: www.museodelprado.es (click on translate for English)

Something Portuguese and Spanish *for* You to Do

Bulls love to eat apples. Can you get the bull through the maze so he can eat some? *The solution is on page 80.*

Letter from
Greece

October 12, 1963

Dear Class:

My wonderful time in Greece started with a serious problem. But you know me, I wouldn't let that stop me from having a good time. I arrived in Athens to find that the hotel I booked could keep me for only one night. The other hotels I was referred to were full. Now what to do? Thinking quickly, I booked a five-day archeological tour around Greece. That way I'd have a place to sleep and also go to places I wanted to visit. Then I arranged for a hotel room when I came back to Athens.

With that settled, I scurried off to the Acropolis, the flat-top rock on a hill looking over Athens that is home to more than twenty ancient buildings. Number one is the Parthenon, built in the fifth century B.C. as a temple to Athena, the goddess of wisdom for whom Athens is named. I knew what it would look like from pictures, but the sheer size of it, plus having the bright blue sky appear between the columns, made the experience especially magical.

I went back to the Acropolis that night to see a performance at the Herod Atticus Theater. The play—Andromache by the fifth-century B.C. writer Euripides—was performed in that very theater when Euripides was alive nearly 2,400 years ago. It was in Greek, so I

Acropolis

Many buildings were constructed on the Acropolis starting as long ago as 6000 B.C. Over the years they were mostly destroyed. The ones Mrs. J saw were built in the fifth century B.C. The Parthenon has forty-six columns going around the outside of the rectangular building. Today, most of the sculptures and other decorative work that were part of the Parthenon and other buildings on the Acropolis are either missing or in museums. Other cities have an Acropolis—which literally means high (*acro*) city (*polis*). The one in Athens is the most famous.

didn't understand a word of it. But I sat at the edge of my stone seat and was so moved by the acting that I wept at the sad story of a woman trying to protect her son. (She does.)

When I started my tour the next day, some of what I saw was based on myth, some of it on events that actually took place. Consider the myth at Delphi, which was the most important shrine in all of ancient Greece. In the old days people came there to seek advice from Pythia, the Oracle at Delphi, who would answer questions about the future—when to plant, when to go to war, whom to marry. If you didn't like her answer, you could get another one, if you left her more gold or other treasures. Do you think she could really tell the future?

Heading south, the next archeological site to visit was Olympia, the seat of the Olympic Games. Starting in 776 B.C., the games, like today, were held every four years. Most of the temples and sporting facilities are in ruins, but the Olympic flame still has a place of honor in front of the Temple of Hera, goddess of love and marriage. Today the flame is carried on a torch by relay—handed to one person, then another—over land and sea to the city where the games are held.

Oracle at Delphi

One of the myths about the Oracle at Delphi is that when she "spoke," smoke came out of the earth. Even Mrs. J looked for the smoke. It turns out that there is some truth behind the story (but not the Oracle telling the future). Greece is in an area of the world where there are earthquakes strong enough to cause cracks in underground rocks. Scientists now believe that gases in the cracked rocks escape and mix with groundwater to form steam that looks like smoke coming out of the ground.

Modern Olympics

When the summer Olympics were held in Greece in 2004, the shot put events for women and men were held in the same stadium where women had once been banned. The Olympics stopped being held in the fifth century A.D. The first modern Olympics were held in Athens in 1896, and the Winter Olympics were added in 1924.

No one lived in Olympia in the old days, but athletes could stay for a six-month training period before an event. Women were not allowed on the grounds, but they could watch the games from a hill overlooking it. If a woman dressed up as a male to sneak into the grounds—even to help a brother or son who was competing—the penalty was very severe and could result in death.

We stopped in Epidaurus, home of the fourth-century B.C. theater that is famous for how well sound travels in it. People in the last row can hear a speaker in the center of the stage as well as those in the front row. There was no performance that day so I climbed up to the top row to test this. It was quite a climb, too, because there are fifty-five rows of seats. Anyway, I could hear what a friend was saying who was standing all the way down in the center of the stage.

When I returned to Athens, I had time to explore the city—the museums, the shops, the street life. For a day trip out of town, I went to Cape Sounion to see the ruins of the Temple of Poseidon and the cliff off which King Aegeus threw himself. (The Aegean Sea is named for him.) Here's how the story goes: Aegeus killed himself in grief because he saw that the boat

Poseidon is the god of the sea, so Cape Sounion is a fitting site for a temple named for him. In ancient days, when sailors saw the white marble columns of the temple, they knew they were close to Athens.

carrying his son Theseus had black sails, a sign that Theseus had been killed by a big monster. However, according to the legend, Theseus was alive and had slain the monster but forgotten to change the sails to white.

I went to the Acropolis again and sat in the shade of the Parthenon and read a book. I've been so busy that I haven't had much time for reading. I also began writing this letter to you. Only a few other tourists were there and it was very peaceful. The city streets, however, are anything but quiet. People are selling, buying, looking, standing, and talking on the streets. Athenians never seem to go home, especially on Sunday when there is a formal changing of the guard at the Presidential Palace. The guards, called Evzones, wear a traditional uniform that looks like a pleated skirt. They also have big pom-poms on their shoes and tassels tied around their legs.

There are more than six thousand Greek islands, and I couldn't leave Greece without going to some of them. Most of the islands have no people living on them. Only seventy-eight of the islands have more than a hundred people as permanent residents. I took a cruise that stopped at four islands-each was different, each was special.

Changing of the guard at
Presidential Palace in Athens

Stone lion in Delos

The first island we stopped at was Delos, the birthplace of Apollo, the god of prophecy and healing. It was second only to Delphi in religious significance, and a lot of people used to live there. Today, only a dozen caretakers and guides live on the island. Tourists cannot spend the night there. Standing guard, as they did in ancient times, are beautiful stone lions.

Close to Delos is Mykonos with its dazzling white houses, 365 churches, windmills, and a lot of tourists. Anyone who visits Mykonos-even for one day like I did-gets to meet Peter the Pelican, the town mascot. He struts about downtown and knows that he is the center of attraction.

Compared to Delos and Mykonos, which you could walk around easily, Rhodes is a huge island. We drove for more than an hour to visit the Acropolis in Lindos. I walked up narrow streets and cobblestone steps to get a bird's-eye glimpse of the fishing boats and the deep blue of the water down in a cove. Little did I know that after a long climb down I would swim in that cove.

The old part of the city of Rhodes has many historic places to visit-from Greek temples to medieval castles. The famed Colossus of Rhodes, a 105-foot-high statue of the sun god Helios built in the third century B.C., toppled long ago. A guide told me that there were

Peter the Pelican

In 1958 a local fisherman found a wounded pelican off the coast of Mykonos. The pelican was nursed to health by the locals and was named Peter (*petro* in Greek means rock or stone). He settled in to become a local himself until he was hit by a car in 1985 and died. He was replaced and now there are three pelicans—including one called Peter. Mrs. J had fun feeding the original Peter bread crumbs.

Santorini's Volcano

The volcanic eruption that took place on Santorini in 1600 B.C. was so violent that the plume from it reduced temperatures around the world. Crops reportedly failed then in China, where there was a frost in July. And tree rings in California, Germany, Ireland, and Sweden show evidence of climate change from thirty-six hundred years ago. The Santorini volcano is now considered dormant. The last eruption took place in 1950.

so many broken pieces that it took the backs of nine hundred camels to take them all away. Even so, I went to the spot where it had stood and imagined what it had looked like, with one huge foot on each side of the harbor.

The island of Santorini is all that is left of a volcano that literally blew up and sank. The sea is in the crater of the volcano, and most of the island is the remaining black rock wall of it. Legend has it that it is the so-called lost continent of Atlantis, but there is no proof that continent even existed. For my last adventure in Greece, I took a bumpy mule ride to the top of the mountain. I can still see the view of the island and sea from there in my mind's eye as I write this letter.

Back in Athens I took a final look at the Acropolis, had a farewell dinner with my friends from the boat, and packed for Turkey, the next stop on my magic carpet ride around the world.

Yassou (pronounced ya-sou) to Greece,

Mrs. J

If You Go to Greece...

- What question would you ask the Oracle at Delphi?

- Which archeological site would you go to first? Mrs. J couldn't wait to see the Acropolis in Athens.

Fun Facts:
Did You Know That...

- The yo-yo, the second oldest known toy in the world (after the doll), was first made in Greece more than three thousand years ago.

- The reason so many doors, window sills, and church domes are painted turquoise—especially on the islands—is that this color is believed to keep evil away. The Greek word for turquoise is *kynos*. Cyanide, a poisonous chemical, comes from this word.

- The saying "take the bull by the horns" comes from a Greek myth. According to the myth, the hero Hercules saved the island of Crete from a bull by grabbing its horns and wrestling it to the ground. What do you think this saying means?

- An old-fashioned way of proposing to a girl in Greece is to toss her an apple. If this were done today, do you think the girl might toss it right back...or eat it?

Check Out What Mrs. J Saw: AN ONLINE TOUR

Acropolis: www.stoa.org/athens/sites/acropolis.html
Colossus of Rhodes: www.awhistory.com/sevenwonders/
    colossus.html
Epidaurus: www.grisel.net/epidaurus.htm
Oracle at Delphi: www.ancient-greece.org/history/delphi.html
Temple of Poseidon: www.sacred-destinations.com/greece/
    temple-of-poseidon-sounio

Something Greek *for* You to Do

Write Your Name in Greek

The Greek alphabet has been used for more than twenty-five hundred years. Even though it is different from ours, we get the word alphabet from the first two letters of the Greek alphabet: alpha and beta. Write your name in Greek by copying the letters in the chart below. The first symbol is the letter in uppercase (capital letters); the second is in lowercase.

GREEK ALPHABET

Letters	English Sound	Name	Letters	English Sound	Name
A α	a	alpha	N ν	n	nu
B β	b	beta	Ξ ξ	x	xi
Γ γ	g	gamma	O o	o	omicron
Δ δ	d	delta	Π π	p	pi
E ε	e	epsilon	P ρ	r	rho
Z ζ	z	zeta	Σ σ	s	sigma
H η	e	eta	T τ	t	tau
Θ θ	th	theta	Y υ	y,u	upsilon
I ι	i	iota	Φ φ	f	phi
K κ	k	kappa	X χ	kh	chi
Λ λ	l	lambda	Ψ ψ	ps	psi
M μ	m	mu	Ω ω	o	omega

Letter from
Turkey

October 17, 1963

Dear Class:

  After moving from one place to another in Greece, my time in Turkey was quite a contrast: I stayed in one city, Istanbul. It is the only city in the world that spans two continents-Europe on one side of the Bosporus Strait and Asia on the other.

  As in Greece, I had a problem with my hotel when I first arrived, but this time it wasn't because there wasn't a room. I found a room, all right, but it was dirty. When I complained, I got a beautiful room with a balcony facing the water. I certainly have learned to speak out for myself on this trip. I was given a dirty room on one of my weekend trips in France, but I stayed in it anyway.

  I've also learned that traveling alone doesn't really mean you are alone. On a half-day bus tour around Istanbul, I met five people I knew from earlier in my trip, including some from the Greek island boat.

  The tour featured two famous mosques. The first was built in the sixteenth century for Suleiman the Magnificent. Isn't that a fantastic-or should I say magnificent-name? Suleiman was the longest-ruling sultan of the Ottoman Empire and could build whatever he wanted. (Sultan is what the head of a Moslem country

The Suleiman Mosque was finished in 1557. It was damaged by a fire in 1660, by an earthquake in 1766, and by another fire during World War I when the courtyard was used to store ammunition that ignited. It was rebuilt in 1956, so Mrs. J saw the mosque in its former splendor.

Over the years, Istanbul had many names. It was called Byzantium by Greeks who settled there in the seventh century B.C. They named it after their king, Byzas. For a very long time it was called Constantinople, after the fifth-century A.D. Roman emperor Constantine. In 1930, the city was officially renamed Istanbul, which comes from the Greek word *istanpolis—* to go to the city. A popular song in 1953 was "It's Istanbul (not Constantinople)."

The Blue Mosque has six minarets or towers, while most mosques have fewer. Here's why: the sultan asked the architect to build a mosque with gold minarets. Gold in Turkish is *altin*. The architect thought he said *alti,* which is six in Turkish. The architect was lucky because the sultan liked the design. He wasn't pleased with the work of the previous architect and had him killed.

was called, just like we call the head of our country president. Suleiman was the sultan for forty-six years.) The second was the Blue Mosque, which has twenty thousand blue mosaic tiles on the ceiling. Its proper name is the Sultanahmet Mosque.

The sultans lived in Topkapi Palace for nearly four hundred years—from the fifteenth to the nineteenth centuries. In addition to the palace, there are smaller buildings on the site, including mosques, bakeries, and a mint where coins were made. At one point, as many as four thousand people lived or worked there. Topkapi is now a museum that houses beautiful items that belonged to the sultans. One of the gold thrones I saw was decorated with more than twenty-five thousand pearls. The dinner-party dishes were displayed in the former kitchen, which was large enough to cook for three thousand guests. It took four men just to lift and empty a pot of soup. I wonder how many people it took to clean up after a party.

Speaking of food, I had lunch in the Spice Bazaar, a huge seventeenth-century building. (Bazaars are basically lots of shops in an enclosed area where you bargain for whatever you want to buy. Bazaar means place of prices in Persian. The language is also called

Farsi.) Even though it's named the Spice Bazaar, nuts, honey, and dried fruits are sold there as well. I bought dried mulberries (they taste like raisins), apricots, and dates. The aromas from both the food and the market made everything I ate taste better. I'm collecting recipes from all of the countries I visit and want to share some of them with you and the rest of the students at school. Wouldn't it be fun to have an international food day when I come home!

Istanbul is a city that loves bazaars, and the grandest of all is the Covered Bazaar. What started as a place for merchants to store and sell merchandise in the fifteenth century grew into a maze of more than three thousand small shops. One of the shops I stopped at sold evil eye beads, which are supposed to ward off bad spirits. They are called evil eyes because they look sort of like eyeballs. I bought a belt with two evil eyes and a necklace with about two dozen eyes looking everywhere.

For a trip to the Asian side of the city, I took a boat ride on the Bosporus. (I can't believe that I'll be in Asia soon and for a lot longer than a day trip.) The boat went past large homes from the olden days as well as small fishing villages. One place of historical interest I saw from the boat was the Selimiye Barracks

The Covered Bazaar has more than sixty streets. Without a map, it is very easy to get lost. There are sections for different products—jewelry, hats, clothes, books, and more. If it looks like you are going to buy something, the salesperson has a helper rush off to get you coffee. After stopping in a couple of shops, Mrs. J and her friend tried to say no to another cup of coffee, but saying no is considered rude. They ended up drinking a lot of coffee.

Mrs. J at the Spice Bazaar

Evil eye beads go back thousands of years. The earliest written mention of them is on clay tablets from 3000 B.C. The traditional Turkish bead is blue and the so-called white eye on it stares back at the world to keep you safe from harm. Some people think blue represents the good fortune associated with water, which makes things grow. Today you can buy evil eye beads in many colors.

41

Florence Nightingale was called "the lady with the lamp" because she visited the sick soldiers at night during the Crimean War between the Russians and the British, French, and Turks (1853–56). She put modern nursing methods into practice, some as simple as keeping patients clean and providing sanitary conditions in the hospital.

where Florence Nightingale nursed British soldiers during a war that took place there in the mid-1800s. She became famous for saving hundreds of soldiers' lives. On my next trip to Istanbul, I'll make sure to visit this museum. Here I am on a six-month trip around the world, and I still don't have time to do everything.

One day I took a trolley and then a ferry to visit a private American school where a friend of mine teaches. Children are required to go to school in Turkey, but the law is not enforced because there aren't enough schools. A young woman working as a waitress in my hotel, for example, could read and write, but she went to school only through the second grade.

The school I visited has six hundred students. The science room is in an old cistern—a huge space for storing water in the years before pipes were built to bring water into a building. Mira, the art teacher, invited me to have tea in her cottage, which has a view of the Bosporus. In her garden there were two pomegranate trees with ready-to-pick fruit. I took one to eat later.

Following a map that Mira drew on the back of an envelope, I walked down an alley and through some crowded streets to the ferry. A young woman, who spoke only Turkish, became my friend on the

Turkish Mosaics

The art teacher in the school Mrs. J visited was giving her students a lesson in how to make Turkish mosaics. A mosaic is a design or picture made from a lot of small, usually square pieces of colored glass or stone. Popular colors for mosaics in Turkey are turquoise and blue. While some of the students did a very good job, none came near the complicated design of the mosaic wall tiles in the Topaki Palace. One section of these tiles is pictured at the right.

boat. We used hand motions to talk and somehow we understood each other. When we landed, she realized I wanted to take a cab to my hotel and offered to help me get one.

And this is when the fun began. She asked a policeman who was directing traffic to find a cab. He left his post, looked around and told me to go to the parked car across the street. I got into it, even though it was packed with a group of young men coming home from soccer practice. They didn't seem to want me to get in, but in I went. In Turkey-and other places I've been on this trip-people share cabs, so I didn't think anything about joining them. When the driver dropped me off at the hotel, he wouldn't accept any money. It turns out that I forced my way into a private car, not a shared taxi. As I was leaving, one of the young men asked my name. I said, "Mrs. United States." What a fun way to leave Istanbul. I wonder what adventures await me in Israel, my next stop.

<u>Hoşçakal</u> (pronounced hoash-cha-kull) to Turkey,

Mrs. J

If You Go to Turkey...

- What would you want to buy in the Spice or Covered Bazaar in Istanbul?

- Would you like to visit a school, like Mrs. J did? You could meet kids in your grade and find out what their classes are like.

Fun Facts:
Did You Know That...

- It is believed that Noah's Ark landed on Mount Ararat in eastern Turkey.

- People in ancient Anatolia in central Turkey were the first to use writing. Clay tablets found there date back to 1950 B.C. Each year, there are more than 150 archeological expeditions underway in Turkey looking for more hidden treasures.

- Santa Claus didn't come from the North Pole. St. Nicholas, who became popular as Father Christmas or Santa Claus, was born in Patara on the southern coast of Turkey. He was known for his secret gift giving, especially to poor people.

- The polite way to address a man in Turkey is to use his first name followed by *bey* (pronounced bay). You would call a woman by her first name followed by *hanim* (pronounced ha-num). If you wanted to speak to Mrs. J, you would say Helene Hanum or Teacher Helene Hanum.

Check Out What Mrs. J Saw: AN ONLINE TOUR

Blue Mosque: www.bluemosque.co

Covered Bazaar: www.turkishculture.org/architecture/bazaar-98.htm

Spice Bazaar: culinarytravel.about.com/od/photogalleries/ig/Spice-Bazaar-Istanbul-/

Suleiman Mosque: www.sacred-destinations.com/turkey/istanbul-suleiman-mosque

Topkapi Palace: www.topkapipalace.com

Something Turkish *for* You to Do

Make Noah's Pudding

When food was about to run out on the ark, it is said that Noah mixed and cooked all that he had left. The result: Noah's Pudding. It is called *asure* (pronounced ashure) in Turkish.

Here's how to make one:

Ingredients

1 cup barley
I cup canned chickpeas, washed and drained
1 cup canned white kidney beans, washed and drained
1 cup sugar
1 teaspoon vanilla extract
10 cups water
10 dried apricots, soaked in water overnight, cut in pieces
10 dried figs, cut in pieces
½ cup raisins
Topping: ¼ cup crumbled walnuts and seeds of ½ pomegranate

Instructions

1. Put 4 cups of water in a large pot, along with the barley. Bring to a boil on high heat.

2. Add the chickpeas, beans, sugar, vanilla, apricots, figs, raisins, and 6 cups of hot water.

3. Cook for about 45 minutes on medium-low heat. Stir occasionally.

4. Pour into a bowl and let cool.

5. Refrigerate. Serve cold or at room temperature. When serving, put crumbled walnuts and pomegranate seeds on top.

October 27, 1963

Dear Class:

Moving from some of the oldest countries in the world, I came to one of the newest. Israel was founded just fifteen years ago, in 1948. Even though it is a new country, it has a very old history. In Jerusalem I went to places mentioned in the Bible. Mt. Zion Church is where it is said that the Last Supper took place. The room directly above it holds King David's tomb.

Mt. Zion is one of several hills in Jerusalem. I climbed to the top and have a pin saying I did so. It was so hot on the way up that I felt like I was in an oven. More to my liking were the stained-glass windows at the synagogue at Hadassah Hospital. Designed by the Russian artist Marc Chagall, who paints on Jewish themes, each window represents one of the twelve tribes of Israel, and all are in brilliant colors. And I mean brilliant—yellow, red, orange, green, and a lot of blues. I went back a few hours later to look at the windows when the sun was shining through different ones from in the morning. It was truly stunning and a wonderful way to end the day.

I used Tel Aviv as my home base and took trips from there. One day I went to Haifa, a seaport built on

Mt. Zion Myths

Mt. Zion Church was built in the twelfth century, so if this is where the Last Supper took place, it clearly had to be in a different building on or near the same site. As for the Tomb of David, it is highly unlikely that he is actually buried there. According to the Bible, King David was buried on an eastern hill on the other side of Jerusalem. Another report from fourth-century pilgrims has him buried in Bethlehem. No matter what's true, Mt. Zion is a popular place to visit for both Christians and Jews.

Stained-glass window by Chagall
in Jersusalem

45

Mrs. J never got to travel around the world by ship, but she did go across the Pacific Ocean and stopped in Samoa, Tahiti, New Zealand, Australia, and other places. Traveling by ship, she said, means you can travel without packing and unpacking every time you go to a new place.

Beersheba, which was founded by Israelites a thousand years before Christ, is mentioned in the Bible. It is where Abraham and Isaac built wells. There are many ruins from those days. You can actually see how the city was laid out with streets, houses, and other buildings.

the slope of Mt. Carmel and about an hour's drive from Tel Aviv. The harbor was very busy the day I was there with ships from all over the world. Maybe next time I go around the world, I'll go by ship.

Halfway between Haifa and Tel Aviv is Caesarea, an old Roman city built by King Herod in the first century B.C. and named for Caesar Augustus. It was a major city back then. Today it is a suburb for people working in Haifa or Tel Aviv. It has a lot of archeological ruins, including special bridges called aqueducts that brought water from Mt. Carmel and an amphitheater that could seat twelve thousand people. I walked on the beach and sifted through the sand looking for archaeological remains. I didn't find any pieces of pottery or coins, but it was fun to think that I might have.

Israel is a small country, so it is easy to get to visit a lot of different places. The first stop on a multiday tour was Beersheba in the Negev Desert. I had never been to a desert and expected to see only sand. While parts of it were just sand, other areas had colorful plants in bloom, including a bright red-orange local tulip.

In contrast to life in the desert, the Dead Sea is really dead. It is the lowest point on earth—thirteen

Mrs. J at the Roman aqueduct in Caesarea

46

Nazareth

There are many sites associated with Jesus in Nazareth, including Mary's Well, the place where Mary and Jesus went to draw water. The well Mrs. J saw was built in the nineteenth century over the original one.

Camels at a taxi stand in Nazareth

hundred feet below sea level—and nothing can live there. It is beautiful in a ghostly way—a greenish, smelly sea surrounded by dead-looking mountains. The water is very salty—much saltier than the oceans—and it is believed to have healing qualities. Some people soak in the water to relieve aches and pains; others go in for a swim. I only dunked my feet, but they felt great afterwards.

On the way north to Nazareth I saw many Bedouins in villages and on the road with their herds of goats and sheep. I waved to them; they waved back. Nazareth is where Jesus was born. Back then, about five hundred people lived in Nazareth. Today, even though it is a busy modern city, I saw a camel waiting in front of a taxi stand.

The Sea of Galilee—also known as Lake Kinneret or Lake Tiberias—was a welcome change from the Dead Sea. It is blue and beautiful and, as Israel's largest reservoir of drinking water, is a source of life. It is also popular with Israelis—and with tourists like me—as a vacation place. We went to nearby Capernaum, which has Roman ruins as well as early Christian churches and Jewish synagogues. I particularly liked a Roman olive press made of stone. The people I saw in Capernaum were living as in olden days. I saw a group of women

Bedouins are Palestinian Arabs who lived a nomadic life for thousands of years, going from place to place with their herds. By the time Mrs. J was in Israel, most Bedouins lived in villages, farmed the land, and had TVs, modern plumbing, and other comforts of modern life.

Ancient olive press in Capernaum

Schools are air conditioned in Israel now, so children in Tel Aviv have school even in hot weather. Which would you prefer: air conditioning in school or having a day or two off because it's so hot?

grinding wheat by hand and two donkeys pulling heavy farm equipment.

My last excursion in Israel brought me down to Eilat—the southern tip of Israel on the Gulf of Aqaba in the Red Sea. I flew down on an old bumpy plane. The alternative was an old bumpy bus through the desert. The plane was quicker and it gave me a great view of the desert scenery below. It was 95 degrees when I was there, but with low humidity (about 8 percent) it was actually bearable. Schools stay open in Eilat even when it reaches 110 degrees. I was told that in Tel Aviv schools close when it hits 85 because the humidity is so much higher there that it feels hotter.

I had planned to spend part of my last day in Israel on the beach in Tel Aviv. However, it was so muggy that I went to the airport earlier than necessary to catch a plane to India just to be able to be in an air-conditioned place.

Shalom (pronounced sha-lome) to Israel,

Mrs. J

48

If You Go to Israel...

- Have you ever been in a desert? You'll have a chance to go to one in Israel since more than 60 percent of the country is desert. As Mrs. J learned, there's a lot more than sand there.

- You can ski in the Golan Heights in the north, snorkel in Eilat in the south, or walk along beaches in Tel Aviv and Haifa. What outdoor activity would you like to do in Israel?

Fun Facts: Did You Know That...

- In Israel, chocolate milk comes in a small plastic bag just big enough for one serving. Chocolate milk comes in other types of containers, but any Israeli kid will tell you that the tastiest—and the most fun—way to drink it is out of a bag. For a different taste sensation, you can also buy banana milk in a bag.

- Sesame Street puppets in Israel speak Hebrew, Arabic, and Russian. A cousin of Oscar the Grouch is Moishe Oofnik.

- Even if you don't follow Jewish food laws (called keeping kosher), in Israel you are stuck with them—literally. The glue on the back of stamps is approved by rabbis as being kosher.

- There is a biblical zoo in Jerusalem, but it has a lot more than two of each kind of animal that went aboard Noah's ark. It was set up to have only wildlife mentioned in the Old Testament, but it now has twenty-two hundred animals representing some three hundred species, including many that are endangered.

Check Out What Mrs. J Saw: AN ONLINE TOUR

Beersheba: www.bibleplaces.com/beersheba.htm
Chagall Windows: www.hadassah-med.com/about/art-at-hadassah/chagall-windows.aspx
Caesarea: www.jewishvirtuallibrary.org/jsource/vie/Caesarea.html
Dead Sea: www.jewishvirtuallibrary.org/jsource/vie/Deadsea.html
Nazareth: www.sacred-destinations.com/israel/nazareth

Something Israeli *for* You to Do

ISRAELI Word Search

Q	O	A	I	N	D	C	F	M	S	G	N	T	B	T
H	E	V	J	V	X	E	I	F	V	X	N	Y	X	T
G	A	L	I	L	E	E	B	L	F	K	B	Q	H	T
O	T	A	E	R	A	S	E	A	C	I	M	N	A	C
B	E	E	R	S	H	E	B	A	B	E	S	L	A	Q
S	S	H	W	B	B	C	B	L	L	N	I	P	O	E
S	K	O	U	K	W	E	E	A	S	E	E	U	S	N
V	U	F	A	G	W	Z	S	O	K	R	X	R	A	I
R	D	I	O	B	L	U	G	Q	N	H	I	L	D	U
R	A	E	R	L	R	D	Q	A	Z	Q	Y	W	H	O
M	N	V	W	E	Q	S	U	M	S	P	P	D	A	D
W	P	P	J	A	B	M	A	G	D	B	J	D	I	E
A	P	S	F	R	L	I	M	V	E	G	E	N	F	B
O	Z	D	T	S	D	K	T	G	W	N	T	T	A	B
V	Y	I	H	I	H	W	P	A	Z	L	E	F	V	I

Find these hidden words in the grid.

They can be horizontal, vertical, or diagonal—frontward or backward. Mrs. J saw things related to everything on this list. *The solution is on page 80.*

BEDOUIN	GALILEE
BEERSHEBA	HAIFA
BIBLE	ISRAEL
CAESAREA	JERUSALEM
CAPERNAUM	NEGEV
EILAT	TIBERIUS

Letter from
India

November 10, 1963

Dear Class:

I've been to a number of countries by now and thought I was an experienced traveler. But nothing prepared me for India. Being in India is like being in a totally new world.

Cows roam about city streets. They are allowed to walk everywhere because Hindus consider them a source of life so they are not killed. (Cows are used for milk and cheese but their meat is not eaten.) Wild monkeys, too, run across the busy streets. Almost all of the women wear traditional Indian saris—a long cloth draped around the body in a special way. (At first I felt out of place not wearing one but then got used to looking different.) Young children—mostly boys—crowd the streets selling grapefruit, newspapers, and shoe shines. They are barefoot and polite, and I couldn't say no to them. As a result I had a lot of grapefruit in my room.

Indian cities sound different, too. All cities are noisy, but here the streets are so crowded with people that there is a throbbing noise like a beating drum that never stops.

Deciding what to visit in Delhi was difficult because there were so many interesting things to see. Jantar

Hindu Symbol

Cows as well as people often wear a tilak—a mark made of powder or paste on the forehead. It is a Hindu symbol of good fortune.

Schools became free in India only in 2010. When Mrs. J was there, people had to pay to send their children to school. Poor children couldn't afford to go, which is why she saw so many boys on the street. Today, children ages 6–14 are required to go to school.

51

Delhi had a population of 2.3 million people when Mrs. J was there. Today it has 17.8 million people. Calcutta and Mumbai have even more people. India has the second-largest population in the world—1.3 billion people; China has 1.4 billion.

Mantar, also called the Delhi Observatory, is a collection of stone and marble structures for measuring the longest and shortest days of the year, tracking the movement of planets, and more. It was built in the eighteenth century by Maharaja Jai Singh II, the ruler of Jaipur in central India who was also an astronomer and a mathematician. You might think that an observatory would be in a quiet place where people can study the stars, but this one is downtown in crowded, noisy Delhi.

The highlight in Delhi for me was the Red Fort built in the seventeenth century by Emperor Shah Jahan. There are palaces, meeting halls, a mosque, and a drum house where musicians played for the emperor and visiting royalty. I saw marble everywhere-on the floors, walls, fountains, and arches. The marble bath house is so big that more than 120 pounds of wood were burned to make enough hot water for the emperor's tub.

I took a tour into the countryside and saw first-hand some of the different ways of life in India. We passed through mud villages with houses topped with thatched roofs. The houses were very picturesque, but I don't think you would like living in one of them. They have no electricity or running water.

Red Fort

The marble arches in the Red Fort were designed to be perfect. Mrs. J learned that if a workman made a mistake in carving, he was beheaded. The place where lion and elephant fights took place in the old days is now a dusty field for street performers. The only animal Mrs. J saw was a cow.

Mrs. J on an elephant in Jaipur

Women were washing clothes in the river, using sticks to beat them clean, and children were playing in the water. Barbers were giving haircuts on the street, men were sitting under a tree, and swarms of people were everywhere. The tour leader said about village life: "No one in India is lonely."

A fair was going on in a nearby town, and hundreds of people wearing clothes in every color of the rainbow were walking on the road to it. Cooked food was for sale—sweet beans, meat, and vegetable patties. There was more stuff to sell than I could imagine, from clothes and plastic dishes to false teeth. The mud villages don't have shops, so a fair like this one is where people can buy things they need.

In Jaipur, I took an elephant ride and found it much easier than the donkey ride in Santorini or the ski lift in Capri. The elephants were decorated with colorful scarves hanging from each ear, and their faces, trunks, and tusks were painted in elaborate designs. Everything in Jaipur is colorful, especially the buildings, which are mostly pink. You will not be surprised to learn that it is nicknamed the Pink City. It was once the capital for royalty so there are a lot of palaces here. I visited one and saw bridal gowns that had so many jewels sewn on them that a bride couldn't walk wearing one. She had to be carried into her wedding.

The Taj Mahal was built in the seventeenth century by Emperor Shah Jahan as a memorial to his favorite wife, Mumtaz Mahal, who is buried there. This is the same emperor who built the Red Fort in Delhi and the Gardens of Shalimar in Srinagar. The Taj Mahal is a mausoleum—an above-ground building for the dead. When Jahan died, his grave was placed by the side of his wife. Built entirely of white marble, the Taj Mahal is especially beautiful at dawn or at sunset, as Mrs. J discovered.

The final stop was such a contrast to the mud villages: the famed, marble Taj Mahal, which is the most exquisite monument I have ever seen. It sits-actually it looks like it's floating-on two marble bases. The lower one is black, the upper one white. I went back after dinner to see it by moonlight, and even though it was only a half-moon, it was totally mysterious. The precious stones decorating the building sparkled, and it looked as if electric lights were shining through tiny holes in the marble.

After a few days back in Delhi, I flew off for another dream trip on my magic carpet to Srinagar in Kashmir, where I spent a few days on a houseboat. This was the first home-like place I stayed in since leaving the United States four months ago. My room was a cozy place with wool blankets made from Kashmir goat hair (we call it cashmere) and a charcoal stove to keep me warm at night. The man who operated the boat lived with his family on a smaller boat that was attached to mine. Attached to that boat was another one used just for preparing food. I ate chicken with yogurt, nuts and dried fruits, lamb curries, and delicious breads that were not like any of the sliced varieties you find in American supermarkets. It was the best food I had in India.

The days were warm, and I sat under a sky-blue umbrella on the deck and had tea. Small boats passed by with people selling fruit, vegetables, and flowers. One day I left the boat to look at the Gardens of Shalimar. They are laid out on three terraces with hundreds of fountains and several man-made waterfalls. The sound of the water was different at each terrace level. It was misty outside, the mountains were hidden by clouds, and there was a quiet, otherworldly feeling about the place.

My final trip in India was to Varanasi, the holy Hindu city on the Ganges River. This is where people come from all over India-some come from all over the world-to spread the ashes of family members who recently died. The town was crowded-what place in India isn't?-and it felt more like a festival than a place for funerals. People were selling flowers, saris, clay masks, and paper toys in the bazaar and in stalls on the streets all day and night.

We went into a place that sold ivory, and the owner invited us back to his home and workshop. To get there, we went through dark, narrow alleys. Even our guide didn't know where we were going. The house had four rooms. One was for carving ivory, one for storing goods, one for the family to eat and sleep

Snake Charmers

Mrs. J saw snake charmers in many places in India. The practice of working with cobras is not as dangerous as it might seem since the snakes usually are defanged. Snake charming was outlawed in 1972 under the Wildlife Protection Act, but you can still see some people doing it on the streets.

About Cremation

For Hindus, cremation is more than a way to dispose of a dead body. It releases the soul from its earthly life. Ghats are wide stone steps leading down to the Ganges River where people cremate loved ones. Some people come to take a holy dip or walk by the ghats and consult astrologers about the future of their lives. About a hundred ghats line the river.

in, and the final one was for the donkey. I think the donkey got the best deal here—a quiet room of its own.

In the morning, we went down to the Ganges to see the ghats, places where people are cremated. Through the fog, I saw two men carrying a body down the steps to the river to be cleansed, then placed on a wood pile. After the body was burned, the ashes were placed in the river. Listening to the guide explain what was going on, it all sounded natural, but I was so hypnotized by what I saw that I could have believed anything.

Calcutta brought me back to reality. There are as many cows in Calcutta as people sleeping on the sidewalk. Men, women, and children try to keep clean by washing in muddy puddles. As I was packing to leave for Burma and Thailand, I kept thinking about the contrasts of life in India—from the poverty on the streets to the glistening Taj Mahal. I will never forget India.

<u>Namaste</u> (pronounced na-ma-stay) to India,

Mrs. J

If You Go to India...

- Would you like to take an elephant ride like Mrs. J did? She said it was uncomfortable at first but then she got used to sitting on top of a nine-foot-tall animal.

- Remember that Indian food can be very spicy. Most tourist places will serve milder food for Americans.

Fun Facts:
Did You Know That...

- Chess was invented in India. The original word for chess in Sanskrit, the language of ancient India, means four members of an army.

- Marigolds are used for decoration in Hindu weddings. They are a symbol of good fortune and happiness.

- Laughing is a healthy thing to do. There are special health laughing clubs in India where people get together to laugh.

- The number system—1, 2, 3, etc.—was invented in India in the first century A.D. In the fifth century, the mathematician-astronomer Aryabhata developed the rules for the digit zero.

Check Out What Mrs. J Saw: AN ONLINE TOUR

Gardens of Shalimar: www.my-kashmir.com/Shalimar.html
Jantar Mantur (Delhi Observatory): www.jantarmantar.org
Red Fort: www.asi.nic.in/asi_monu_tktd_delhi_redfort.asp
Taj Mahal: www.tajmahal.gov.in
Varanasi: www.varanasicity.com/ganges-ghats.html

Something Indian *for* You to Do

Make a Rangoli Design

Rangolis are colorful geometric designs that are painted on the ground in front of houses in India as a sign of welcome. Traditionally, they are "painted" by using colored rice powder. Sometimes, flower petals are added for extra color.

Using this rangoli design, you can:
- trace it and color it with paint or markers and hang it on your bedroom door; or
- enlarge it on a copy machine, trace it on the sidewalk in front of your house, and color it with chalk.

Letter from
Burma and Thailand

Shwedagon Pagoda

The dome or *stupa* of the Shwedagon Pagoda is made up of nearly nine thousand solid gold blocks. It is decorated with more than five thousand jewels, including diamonds, emeralds, and rubies. At the top of the *stupa* is an emerald that captures the sun's rays. Mrs. J saw the dome glistening in the sunlight.

November 18, 1963

Dear Class:

For the first time since I've been in Asia, I felt alone. The crowds disappeared when I left Calcutta. Imagine my surprise when I was the only person on the plane to Burma, and there were only two people on the tour of the capital, Rangoon–Jao Chankul, a man from Thailand, and me.

A lively guide named May led the two of us on the tour. We went to the University of Rangoon library where I saw old Burmese manuscripts written on palm leaves. Other texts were written on paper, cloth, and metal. How exotic and very different from the manuscripts I saw earlier on my trip in London! We also visited the Shwedagon Pagoda, a sacred site that contains many Buddhist relics, including eight strands of Buddha's hair. Mr. Chankul, who is a Buddhist, bought some incense, a package of candles, two flowers, and two paper pinwheels to leave as a special present for Buddha.

I thought I was in for a special treat one night when May made arrangements for me to go to a local outdoor dance performance in the countryside. It started out more as a nightmare than a treat. It rained so hard that I sat on the bus while the performance

Name Changes

Burma was renamed Myanmar in 1989. The capital was moved from Rangoon (now called Yangon) to Naypyidaw (pronounced nay-pee-dough) in 2006. The new capital is the political seat of the country, but Rangoon or Yangon is the economic and cultural hub.

was delayed. When the dance finally began, I realized the dancers were locals-not trained professionals. In fact, most of the people watching the show were relatives of May's who lived in the village. However, the evening did end up as a treat because I realized I had a special experience-seeing life as it actually goes on in a small Burmese village.

When I flew to Bangkok, the capital of Thailand, Mr. Chankul was also on the plane. His wife met him at the airport, and they invited me to have lunch with them. They ordered their favorite food from the menu, which was a good thing because I wouldn't have known what to choose. Everything that came to the table was delicious: a seafood salad, chicken curry, and orange slices floating in sugar water. I went back to their home with them for tea. On their front lawn was a coconut tree. I picked a fresh one from the tree, which they cracked open for me so I could eat it later.

That night I relaxed in my hotel-still full from lunch-and watched TV for the first time since I was in London nearly five months ago. I had a choice between a Thai boxing match or an American detective show. Even though I don't know anything about boxing, I watched it rather than the more familiar American show. Which program would you have chosen?

Bangkok has a lot of Buddhist temples and statues of Buddha in all sorts of positions: standing, sitting, reclining. I went to the Wat Pho or Reclining Buddha Temple, which is the largest Buddhist temple in the city. The gold-plated Reclining Buddha is also the largest Buddha in the country. In a semi-lying down position with his right arm supporting his head, Buddha stretches out to 160 feet-as wide as a football field. In another temple, Wat Traimit, I saw the much smaller but very famous Gold Buddha. It is less than ten feet tall, but because it is solid gold, it weighs more than five tons.

One day I woke up early to visit the famous Floating Market on the <u>Khlongs</u> that are everywhere in Bangkok. <u>Khlongs</u> are canals. No wonder Bangkok is called the Venice of the East. Thousands of families live on the water. Almost every floating house has a birdcage on a pole. That seems like a creative way to keep a pet on a boat. Imagine if you lived on a boat and had to go out to walk a dog!

Another day I left my hotel at 5:30 in the morning to go by train to the ruins in Ayutthaya, the old capital of Siam (the former name of Thailand). Someone at the hotel wrote out instructions in Thai explaining where I wanted to go, which I showed to people along the way. The train passed by villages where people were just

The Gold Buddha, made more than nine hundred years ago, was hidden under plaster to make it look unimportant to the Burmese when they attacked Bangkok in the 1780s. It stayed hidden until 1957 when it was moved to a new temple in Bangkok. The Buddha slipped from the crane that was moving it and the plaster cracked. A monk saw gold behind the crack, and that's how the Gold Buddha was discovered.

Reclining Buddha

Since the Reclining Buddha is so big, it is not surprising that it has enormous feet. Each foot is about fifteen feet long and ten feet high and is decorated in mother-of-pearl with the 108 symbols by which a Buddha is identified, such as flowers, dancers, white elephants, and tigers. In the hallway near the Reclining Buddha are 108 bronze bowls to represent each of these features. For good luck, people leave money in the bowls. See how small Mrs. J looks next to this Buddha.

Most of the canals have been filled in since Mrs. J's trip and are ordinary streets. There still are floating markets in Bangkok, but they are mostly for tourists.

waking up and starting their day. At each station people were selling food. A man with a ten-year old daughter sat next to me. He insisted I sample some of the food he brought with him. The fruit in a sugar cane basket was delicious, but the peanuts were soggy. I threw them out the window when he wasn't looking.

Ayutthaya was once the largest and richest city in Asia. The Burmese destroyed it in 1767, but you can still see some of the hundreds of temples that were built there. One of the strangest-looking ruins is the stone head of Buddha tangled in the roots of a banyan tree. No one knows for sure how this came to be. One theory is that when they destroyed the temples, the Burmese lopped the heads off Buddha sculptures and left them on the ground and a tree grew around this one.

I had planned to go directly back to Bangkok but instead had a spur-of-the-moment adventure. I told the driver of the pedicab that took me to the train station that I had wanted to go to Bang Pa-In, the King's Summer Palace, but didn't have time to do so. He didn't understand me so he put me on a train to go there. Now I was totally on my own. The handwritten instructions in Thai didn't cover this part of the trip. The conductor put a young man on the train in charge of getting me to the palace and back in time for the

A pedicab is a three-wheel bike that pulls a covered sitting area for passengers. When Mrs. J was on her trip, it was the traditional way to get around rural areas in Asia. They were also used in cities. Today, cities are crowded with cars and motorbikes, but tourists still like to take a pedicab because it is something different to do.

next train to Bangkok. All of this happened with the international means of communicating—using hands, pointing, and smiling. I've gotten really good at this since I've been in many places where no one speaks English.

The next day I wanted to see another palace, the Grand Palace in Bangkok, and the Emerald Buddha Temple, which is on the palace grounds. I had a problem. My plane to Hong Kong left at 11:00 in the morning, but the doors to the palace and temple didn't open until 9:30. I convinced the guard to let me at 9:00 and had the whole place to myself. Everything I saw was a feast for the eyes. There is a very fancy bed that every Thai King is required to sleep in for at least a few nights during his reign. Lovely as it was, it looked very uncomfortable. The Emerald Buddha is only twenty-six inches high, but it is made from a single piece of jade. (Emerald in Thai means dark green, not the semiprecious stone). The King is the only person allowed to touch this Buddha. He changes the clothes it wears three times a year—winter, summer, and rainy season. The Buddha was wearing his winter dress—cotton mesh encrusted with precious stones on gold.

<u>Cha-cha</u> in Burmese and <u>Sa-wat-dee</u> to Thailand,

Mrs. J

If You Go to Burma or Thailand...

- Don't forget to take off your shoes when you visit a Buddhist temple.

- Take a ride in a pedicab, even if it is a touristy thing to do. It's a fun way to travel for short distances.

Fun Facts:
Did You Know That...

- Babies in Burma wear a gold thread around their neck or wrist to protect them from evil spirits.

- The official name of Bangkok is very long. Here it is in translation from Thai: Great City of Angels, Repository of Divine Gems, Great Land Unconquerable, Grand and Prominent Realm, Royal and Delightful Capital City Full of Nine Noble Gems, Highest Royal Dwelling and Grade Palace, Divine Shelter, and Living Place of Reincarnated Spirits.

- Popular Thai snacks are fried cockroaches and caterpillars.

- Lucky days in Thailand are the first and sixteenth days of the month. Some people buy lottery tickets only on those days.

Check Out What Mrs. J Saw: AN ONLINE TOUR

Ayutthaya: whc.unesco.org/en/list/576
Emerald Buddha: www.sacred-destinations.com/thailand/bangkok-wat-phra-kaew-emerald-buddha
Khlongs: www.bangkok.com/attraction-waterway/khlongs.htm
Reclining Buddha: www.sacred-destinations.com/thailand/bangkok-wat-pho
Shwedagon Pagoda: www.shwedagon.org

Something Thai *for* You to Do

Make a Batik Cloth

The traditional way to make a batik cloth is to create a design in wax and then dye the cloth. The waxed areas are resistant to the dye. Here's how to do it with washable white glue and paint:

Instructions

1. Make a design on a white T-shirt, pillowcase, or piece of cotton fabric. You can draw it on a piece of paper and then trace it onto the fabric, or you can draw it directly on the fabric.

2. Follow the lines of the design with washable glue either by squeezing it directly from the bottle or using a brush. Let the glue dry for two to three hours.

3. Fill in the entire fabric with one or more colors using fabric or acrylic paint. Add a little water to acrylic paint, because if it is too thick it can chip off the fabric. Let the paint dry for twenty-four hours.

4. When it is completely dry, remove the glue by soaking the fabric in warm water for thirty minutes. If there is still glue on the fabric, soak it longer. The glue will soften the more it soaks. The part of the fabric that was glued—your design—will not have any color on it.

5. Hang the fabric to dry.

6. Now your batik is ready to wear, use as a pillowcase, or put in a frame.

Letter from
Singapore, Hong Kong, and Taiwan

November 29, 1963

Dear Class:

I've dreamed of going to China for so long, and here I am, almost close enough to see it—but I didn't get there. Why? Because China and the United States do not have diplomatic relations and most Americans are not allowed to travel there. But I did get to experience Chinese culture in three different places: Singapore, Hong Kong, and Taiwan. Let me explain.

The country of Singapore is an island (actually, it is sixty-three islands) off the southern part of Malaysia. Not to confuse you, but Singapore is also the name of the capital. Most of the people living in Singapore are Chinese.

A popular place to visit in Singapore is the Tiger Balm Gardens, which has many statues, including one of a very jolly and huge Laughing Buddha. The garden was built in 1937 by brothers who made an herbal mixture in a cream to rub on sore muscles and other aches and pains. They called this product Tiger Balm. In the garden are statues honoring Chinese heroes. One statue is of Wu Song, who is said to have tamed a wild tiger with his hands. Do you think the balm would have helped Wu

Visiting China

Americans have been traveling to China since 1979. Mrs. J was among the first group of American tourists to go there. When she did, she walked on the Great Wall, visited the Forbidden Palace (it was called forbidden because no one could enter or leave without permission from the emperor), took a boat trip on the Yangtze River, and loved being in China so much that she went back again.

The Laughing Buddha and Mrs. J

Song if he got sore muscles from taming the tiger? I don't. Anyway, I bought a bottle of tiger balm but haven't used it yet. I'll let you know when I get back whether I think it works.

The focus of my short visit to Singapore was children. I visited the Children's Library, where storytelling takes place every day and there are no fines for overdue books. I also went to an American school in a beautiful new building. The school principal is interested in getting more teachers from the United States to come and work here. Don't worry; I won't take a job in Singapore. I'll be back soon.

After Singapore, I traveled to Hong Kong, which is also an island. Although most of the people living here are Chinese, China does not control the government. Britain does—just like it has since 1841. Looking down on Hong Kong from the airplane at night, the city looked like a beautiful fairy land with twinkling lights. It was just as lovely from the ground.

One day I went to the fishing village of Aberdeen. Many people live on their fishing boats, which are called junks. It is odd to see these old-fashioned boats in the water and fancy modern high-rise buildings on the shore. I didn't go on a junk, but I did go on a floating

Hong Kong Today

In 1997, Britain gave up its rights to rule Hong Kong. Today, Hong Kong is officially part of China.

65

restaurant and had a wonderful meal. I ate and ate for hours. Later someone told me it was very unusual for a woman to go to a restaurant by herself. Things like that don't bother me because what I'm doing—traveling around the world by myself—is also unusual for a woman to do.

A top tourist site in Hong Kong—and I really mean top—is Victoria Peak. It is the highest point on Hong Kong Island—eighteen hundred feet high. I took a tram ride up it, and from The Peak (as it is popularly called), I could see the city, harbor, and nearby islands. It was a clear, sunny day and everything sparkled.

How sad to think that just one day later—November 22—there was no more sparkle. That was the day President John Kennedy was shot to death. Flags that had flown high in the wind were now at half-mast. Religious services were held all over the city. I was so far away from home at the time of a national tragedy. While I was very sad, I didn't feel alone. Strangers came up to me on the street to tell me how sorry they were for me and for all Americans. A few days later, all of the buildings were closed for the President's funeral, even though it took place halfway around the world in Washington, D.C.

Victoria Peak

In the 1860s, Europeans living in Hong Kong built homes on Victoria Peak, but didn't want to be bothered climbing up. They went up by sedan chairs, which are like wheel-less taxis that are carried on poles by two to four people.

A junk in Hong Kong harbor

66

National Palace Museum

Two years after Mrs. J was in Taiwan, the museums she visited merged and the collections are now housed in the National Palace Museum in Taipei. There are so many pieces of art—bronzes, paintings, books, jewelry, coins, and fans—that only 1 percent is displayed at a time. The rest is in storage. See the jade Chinese cabbage on the left.

The third island I visited was Taiwan, the Republic of China. People from mainland China, which is called the People's Republic of China, moved there in 1949 because they did not want to live in a communist country. They brought many Chinese treasures with them that are displayed in the Palace Museum and the National Central Museum. Many people believe that the Chinese art in these museums is the finest in the world. My favorite piece was a small sculpture-about the size of a hand-of a Chinese cabbage made from a single chunk of jade. It has tiny grasshoppers hidden in the carved leaves.

Wulai is a mountain village in the north famous for its hot springs and waterfalls. I was supposed to cross a bridge to get to a waterfall, but it was washed out in a recent storm. Instead, I walked across a temporary one made of four planks of wood placed close to the water. It was scary because there was fast-moving water under the planks, and I kept thinking I was going to fall into it. I didn't fall and, as with other scary experiences I've had on this trip, I'm glad I conquered my fear. It was drizzling, misty, and magical by the waterfall.

By now I'd seen a lot of Buddhist temples, but I still wanted to see the oldest and most famous one in Taipei-Longshan Temple. Dedicated to the goddess

Longshan Temple

Before Longshan Temple was built in 1838, according to the legend, someone left something on a nearby tree branch that gave off a strange light. Some people say it was a charm, others say it was a lantern. Either way, it was believed that a wish made near the tree would be granted. It became known as a sacred place, which is why the temple was built there.

of mercy and other deities, the temple has fancy wood carvings and other decorations, including dragons. Even the dragons, however, couldn't protect the temple, which was destroyed by an earthquake, a typhoon, and bombs during World War II. Each time disaster struck, the temple was rebuilt.

I've been to a lot of operas in my life, but never one like the one I went to here. The Chinese Cantonese Opera performed a two thousand-year-old story about a beautiful poor girl who is washing clothes at the river when the king comes by and falls in love with her. The story was lovely and the costumes were beautiful, but the music sounded to me like pots banging together. Eastern music is very different from Western music, and my ears couldn't get used to the difference. I left the performance after an hour and walked around the gaily lit streets of Taipei. It was so crowded with people that it felt like a giant party. Maybe it was a going-away party for me because the next day I flew off to Japan.

<u>Baibai</u> to Singapore, Hong Kong, and Taiwan,

Mrs. J

If You Go to Singapore, Hong Kong or Taiwan…

- Check the theater schedule to see if an animated Cantonese opera is being performed. You'll see cartoons on a movie screen instead of performers on stage. Maybe you'll like the music better than Mrs. J did.

- Listen carefully to see if you can hear the difference between Cantonese Chinese spoken in Hong Kong and Mandarin Chinese spoken in Singapore and Taiwan.

Fun Facts:
Did You Know That…

- Taiwan use to be called Formosa. This means beautiful in Portuguese, which is what Portuguese sailors called it in the sixteenth century when they first came there.

- Singapore is a very clean city. One reason is that it is against the law to drop things on the street, including chewing gum. It is even against the law to chew gum in public.

- Every May there is a bun festival on Cheung Chau, an island near Hong Kong. The festival is to honor the god Pak Tai and to thank him for warding off evil spirits. Some people say the buns feed hungry ghosts that live on the island.

- Lucky numbers in Hong Kong are two, three, six, eight, and nine. Unlucky numbers are one, four, and seven. The numbers 4 and 7 are especially unlucky because they sound like the Chinese word for death. What is your lucky number?

Check Out What Mrs. J Saw: AN ONLINE TOUR

Cantonese Chinese Opera: arts.cultural-china.com/en/87Arts322.html
Longshan Temple: www.orientalarchitecture.com/taiwan/taipei/lungshan.php
National Palace Museum: www.npm.gov.tw/en
Tiger Balm Gardens: www.tigerbalmgardens.org/SINGgardens.html
Victoria Peak: www.hk-victoria-peak.com/history_of_victoria_peak.htm

Something Chinese *for* You to Do

Write a Story about Your Chinese Animal Sign

The Chinese calendar has twelve animal signs. Each year is named for one of these animals in a special order. Every twelve years the same animal appears again. Each animal has special characteristics.
What is your animal year? Write a story about you and your animal. The list includes the years your parents and grandparents were born. Do you share an animal with them?

	Birth Year						
Rat	1936	1948	1960	1972	1984	1996	2008
Ox	1937	1949	1961	1973	1985	1997	2009
Tiger	1938	1950	1962	1974	1986	1998	2010
Rabbit	1939	1951	1963	1975	1987	1999	2011
Dragon	1940	1952	1964	1976	1988	2000	2012
Snake	1941	1953	1965	1977	1989	2001	2013
Horse	1942	1954	1966	1978	1990	2002	2014
Ram	1943	1955	1967	1979	1991	2003	2015
Monkey	1944	1956	1968	1980	1992	2004	2016
Rooster	1945	1957	1969	1981	1993	2005	2017
Dog	1946	1958	1970	1982	1994	2006	2018
Pig	1947	1959	1971	1983	1995	2007	2019

Rat: *cheerful, generous, kind*
Ox: *thoughtful, successful, self-assured*
Tiger: *brave, powerful, great friend*
Rabbit: *happy, bright, trustworthy*
Dragon: *honest, full of energy, strong*
Snake: *wise, helpful, successful*
Horse: *popular, cheerful, clever*
Ram: *wise, shy, caring*
Monkey: *funny, talkative, successful*
Rooster: *proud, thoughtful, early riser*
Dog: *good friend, quick to learn, cares about people*
Pig: *smart, popular, brave*

December 23, 1963

Dear Class:

I ended my trip around the world in Japan, but in one way it was just like when I began it in London six months ago: I was under an umbrella. It rained a lot in Japan, but you know rain doesn't stop me from going out. Anyway, it is good for flowers. Wherever I went I saw vases filled with fresh flowers, including in unusual places such as an elevator and the train station. In Tokyo, I took a flower-arranging class and was pleasantly surprised that my arrangement was selected to be displayed at a tea house.

I also went to a special garden that didn't even have flowers. This garden has only bonsai trees. These are very small trees that are kept in pots, not the ground, so their roots never get large. Some are so small they can fit in your hand. Even though they are small, bonsai trees can live for a very long time. One tree in the garden I visited is more than four hundred years old and worth $3 million. Another feature of the garden is a collection of stones in interesting shapes and colors sitting in pans of water. The colors are reflected in the water. We can do this as a class project when I get back.

A Japanese flower arrangement

The Atago Shrine

The Atago Shrine was built in 1603. In the old days, a young Japanese soldier called a samurai rode his horse up the steps of the shrine to give his military leader—the Shogun—some plum blossoms. It is said that the trip took one minute to go up and forty-five minutes to get down. This is because going down steep steps is harder for a horse than going up. Are you faster walking up stairs or down?

Mrs. J moved to California about ten years after this trip, when she retired from teaching. The fortune teller at the Toshogu Shrine was correct. She made many new friends, became a volunteer at an art museum, took courses at a local college, and things went very well for her.

Every tour I took in Japan went to at least one Shinto shrine. Shinto is an ancient Japanese religion. It has traditional rituals and ceremonies but no set system of belief. It is a way of life for many Japanese. Love of nature, for example, is an important Shinto concept. In Tokyo I visited the Atago Shrine, which is famous for its view of the city because it is on a hill. You have to walk up eighty-six very steep steps to get to the shrine. Getting to the top represents success in life. That must mean I am successful because I got to the top.

I got another sign of my success when I had my fortune told at the Toshogu Shrine. For a few pennies, the old fortune teller told me that things would go very well for me if I moved.

While I loved visiting the shrines in Tokyo, going on the subway was a very different experience. So many people push and shove to get in a car that there is an official "pusher." The stations have first-aid booths because, with all the hordes of people passing through, at least some get sick every day and need medical attention. I was told that they rest and when they feel better they push their way (or are pushed) onto a train.

It was a relief to leave the crowded city for a

Tokyo's Subway

Tokyo is the world's most densely populated city. When Mrs. J was there, the population was 16 million. Today, 35 million people live there. While it might seem like all 35 million are trying to get on the subway, only about 8 million travel that way a day. (New York City's subways carry 5 million passengers a day on weekdays.) For the record, the pushers' official title is passenger arrangement staff.

ten-day trip in the countryside. You may think I was tired of seeing Buddhas by now, but I still had to see the Great Buddha of Kamakura, a huge bronze figure cast in 1252. It is about as tall as a four-story building. The Buddha was originally placed in a wooden house that was washed away by a tsunami in the fifteenth century. Ever since then, it has been outdoors.

When I thought about Japan before I came here, the first image that came to mind was the snow-capped Mt. Fuji. I could hardly wait to see it. As it turns out, I had to wait even when I was in Japan. The first time I passed it, when I was on a bus, the fog hid the mountain. When I passed it a day later, I could see all of Mt. Fuji. It was beautiful and looked just like the many images of it that I had seen in photographs, wood-block prints, and silk scrolls.

Part of my travels around Japan were by train in a wonderful double-decker car with huge windows. I almost felt like I was outdoors as I passed rice paddies, strawberry farms, stacks of hay, and small towns. One day I took a five-minute walk from the train to the Mikimoto Pearl Island, where women divers go into the water to bring up oysters with pearls in them—or at least they hope the oysters have pearls. I bought $5

Mrs. J at the Great Buddha of Kamakura

Diving for pearls

The Inland Sea
is the body of water touching three of the main islands that make up Japan—Honshu, Shikoku, and Kyushu. Overall, Japan has more than three thousand islands.

worth of oysters in which I found a few good pearls. I don't know what I'll do with them, but for now I'll keep them as a souvenir.

A big treat for me was going to the Inland Sea, which is one of the most beautiful parts of Japan. The boat I was on had a large room with wide windows so people could see the changing scenery outside. It was so foggy when I was there that it was hard to see anything clearly, but I could make out mysterious-looking mountain peaks and pine trees on the islands. Children who live on the islands go to school on a ferry. How would you like to do that-especially on a foggy day?

Sometimes I had a private cabin and used the boat as a floating hotel, and sometimes I stayed on land in ryokans-Japanese inns. At the inn in Takamatsu, I probably will be remembered there as "that absentminded American lady." What I was absentminded about was when and where to wear the slippers provided by the innkeeper. I knew that I had to leave my shoes at the door to my room, but sometimes I forgot to put on slippers and walked barefoot. Once I forgot to change into bathroom slippers, and perhaps even worse, I forgot to change out of my bathroom slippers and wore them in the main part of the inn.

Ryokan is the name for a traditional Japanese inn. Each room has a sliding door, a tatami-mat floor, and a futon for sleeping. Tatami mats are traditionally made from rice straw. There is usually a small table for making tea. Guests take off their shoes before walking into the room and walk on the tatami mat, as Mrs. J learned. Another traditional feature of a *ryokan* is common bathing areas—one for men, one for women. Guests are usually given a special kimono bathrobe to wear.

I stayed at a <u>ryokan</u> in Kyoto that was recommended by someone I met in Istanbul. Otherwise, I would not have known about it. (I got great tips from other travelers.) Instead of being in the downtown tourist area, the inn was in a neighborhood where I saw people going to work, shopping, going to school, and doing ordinary everyday activities. I felt like I was their neighbor for the few days I spent there.

Kyoto is a beautiful city and is much smaller and easier to travel around than Tokyo. It was the capital of Japan until 1868, when Tokyo became the capital. The old Imperial Palace is in the center of the city in a lovely park with lots of trees. The leaves were all yellow and red-lovely autumn colors, even though it was winter.

I went to the Nijo Castle, which was built in the sixteenth century by the Tokugawa Shogun. The walls are painted gold with images of tigers. I was surprised that such a fancy place had squeaky floors. The guide told me that because the shogun was afraid of being killed, he had noisy floors designed so his guards could hear if someone was sneaking into the castle.

Kabuki is a special kind of Japanese theater with dancing, acting, and pantomime. Lucky for me, the best

A kabuki play

Kabuki players come to Kyoto in December. They enact traditional stories, so everyone in the audience knows what is going on—except for me. I could follow the story anyway because the performers were so good. The play was about a chief warrior and the battles he fought. He was sitting on a real horse.

Back in Tokyo, on my last day I visited a school where I sat in on two classes: woodworking and music. The students were well-behaved in the classroom but were noisy—very noisy—in the halls. At recess, the kids played jump rope, went on the swings, and ran in the playground, just like you do. It was a whirlwind day and the end of a whirlwind trip.

Sayonara (pronounced sy-o-na-ra) to Japan and hello to the U.S.,

Mrs. J

If You Go to Japan...

- Take the subway in Tokyo. It's an experience you'll never forget. If you don't like crowds, walk or take a taxi instead.

- You can slurp noodles when eating in Japan. It is not considered rude. In fact, it is a sign that you think the noodles taste good.

Fun Facts:
Did You Know That...

- In Japan the traffic light to indicate GO is called blue, even though it is green. This is because long ago green was thought to be a shade of blue.

- Your hairstyle can tell a lot about you in Japan. Some men shave their heads as a form of apology; some women cut their hair after they break up with a boyfriend.

- A popular pizza in Japan has mayonnaise, corn, and seaweed toppings. If you think this sounds yucky, you can also get an American-style one with cheese.

- A traditional way to greet a person is to bow, but be careful if you do this. There are reports of people getting a concussion from bowing too close to each other.

Check Out What Mrs. J Saw: AN ONLINE TOUR

Imperial Palace, Kyoto: sankan.kunaicho.go.jp/english/guide/kyoto.html

Kabuki: www.kabuki-bito.jp/eng/top.html

Kamakura Buddha: www.sacred-destinations.com/japan/kamakura-great-buddha

Nijo Castle: www.japan-guide.com/e/e3918.html

Toshogu Shrine: www.uenotoshogu.com/about/

Something Japanese *for* You to Do

Flower Arranging

Ikebana is a special style of Japanese flower arranging that goes back to the fifteenth century. This is the flower-arranging technique that Mrs. J learned in Tokyo.

You can do it by following these steps:

1. Cut three flower stems or branches into different lengths—short, medium, and long.

2. Fill a bowl halfway with water and place a frog—a spiked holder for cut flowers—in the center. You can also use a vase.

3. Put the longest stem or branch near the center. Lean it slightly to the left side at about a fifteen-degree angle.

4. Put the medium-length stem or branch near the bottom on the left. Place this at a forty-five-degree angle.

5. Put the shortest stem or branch near the bottom on the right. Lean it away from the longest branch at a seventy-five-degree angle.

6. If you want to, add more flowers and branches, but make sure that the total is an odd number. For example, add two stems to the basic arrangement so there are five altogether.

In the End

Mrs. J's dream trip around the world is over. Her magic carpet ride came to an end. What a trip is was! She got to places she had read about for years and saw many famous buildings and pieces of art. She slept in houseboats and inns, heard dozens of different languages, and ate all sorts of food, from fish and chips in London to raw fish in Japan. She learned about different cultures and also a lot about herself. If she could take trains and buses in parts of the world where most people didn't speak English and still get to her destination, she learned that she could do almost anything she wanted to do.

As good as her trip was, six months was a long time to be away, and Mrs. J was glad to return to the United States. The best part of coming home, she said, was being greeted at the airport in New York by her class. "I took dozens of planes over the past six months and no one met me at any airport," she said. "But when I arrived in New York, there were my students waiting for me with a big banner that said: "Welcome Home, Mrs. J."

Back in the classroom she shared two kinds of travel stories with her students: her own adventures and folktales from every country she went to. This way, Mrs. J and her students could always travel somewhere.

What do you think Mrs. J did next?

Planned another trip.

England Word Search (p. 9)

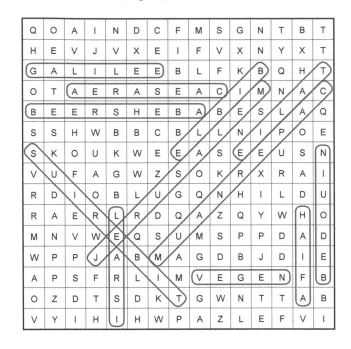

Israeli Word Search (p. 50)

Portuguese-Spanish Maze (p. 31)

About the Author and the Illustrator

Jane J. Stein loves to travel, and like Mrs. J, she has been to every continent except Antarctica. She lives in Washington, D.C., and like Mrs. J, she loves going to museums and operas. Have you guessed that Mrs. J is her mother? She is. Jane goes to Steamboat Springs, Colorado, to ski in the winter and hike in the summer. She spent many years as a journalist and editor and has written two books and hundreds of articles on health. *Dear Class* is her first children's book. She is married and has two children and five grandchildren.

Pamela A. Duckworth also loves to travel. She went to school in France and traveled around Europe just a few years after Mrs. J did, visiting many of the same sites. Pam was a lawyer with firms in Boston, Massachusetts, for 37 years until retiring in 2012. She has always liked to draw and paint and has taken many art classes, starting in grade school and continuing to the present. She lives in Steamboat Springs, Colorado, with her partner, Steve, and her cats, Muddy and Buddy. Pam runs, bikes, and skis when she isn't reading, traveling, or making art.

CPSIA information can be obtained at www.ICGtesting.com
Printed in the USA
BVOW10s1328060914

365792BV00002B/2/P